"Reading *Erasing America* will probably make your blood run cold. It's scary to look at how far away we've moved from our original goals of freedom and independence.

It doesn't matter which side of the political or ideological spectrum you fall, Rodger highlights important issues that everyone who is concerned about the future of America should consider. There's a reason why America has had such a global impact and has been such an attractive destination (whether you think that is a positive or negative thing) for the past few centuries. This book describes how close we are to losing that status and offers practical strategies for returning to our founding values."

Debra Hilton, ghostwriter, direct response copywriter, magnetic marketing strategist

"Rodger Friedman has hit a much-needed home run with his new book *Erasing America: Broken Politics, Broken Country.* His book reminds us that we are in control of our government. Our elected officials *work* for us. They do not have the power to control us, unless we allow them to do so. Each chapter presents a hard-hitting truth about the current state of our Union, our society, and our values. We have lost nearly all connection to the strong and prosperous nation that we were established to be and have wandered far away from those truths that our founders said were self-evident.

Freidman's book reminds us that we must stop the financial bleeding and reverse the course our politicians currently have us on or we will no longer have a nation. His statement that America is "acting like a drunken teenager who stole his mom's credit card and has gone on a spending spree" is spot on. He reminds us that our Freedom is fragile and on the verge of collapsing. Most importantly he shares the fact that "what we tolerate we get more of."

He encourages like-minded folks to become part of a "virtuous circle" who step up to save and not the current vicious cycle that is hell-bent on destroying our Great Nation from the inside out. Each chapter gives us many valid points to consider and ways to work at a local level to enact change. His use of humor and storytelling makes the content come alive and this book has sparked a deeper incentive for me to get off the sidelines and into the battle to save our Republic. Highly recommend this great book!"

Tricia JOY Johnson, founder of Get Back2Basics

"What a book! Rodger Friedman is fearless in his presentation of the *truth* about America today and the degradation of our society happening *now*. He reminds us why America is and always has been the best place to live in all the world—why else would so many people want to live here and try to get here anyway that they can? This is a wake-up call and a must-read for everyone who has the guts to speak up and stand up for our country. It was once great and can be great again if we get moving and take up the call using many of the solutions that Rodger suggests.

Read and re-read this book and then send a copy to those you love, those you respect, fellow conservatives, and yes, send it to those whose opinions you dislike and those you distrust. Pray that their eyes and hearts will be open to remembering the values and truths this country was built on and what it means to be *free*."

Lily Noon, president, Noon International, Inc.

ERASING AMERICA

ERASING AMERICA
BROKEN POLITICS, BROKEN COUNTRY

RODGER FRIEDMAN

Published by EOCritic LLC

ISBN (paperback): 978-0-9996414-4-6

Author photo by Mike Ossola Photography
Book design and production by www.AuthorSuccess.com

Printed in the United States of America

Other Books by Rodger Friedman

Forging Bonds of Steel: How to Build a Successful and Lasting Relationship with Your Financial Advisor

Fire Your Retirement Planner: YOU! Concise Advice on How to Join the $100,000 Retirement Club

The Mindset of Retirement Success: 7 Winning Strategies to Change Your Life

Parent's Guide to Your Child's Retirement: 21 Thought-Provoking Conversations to Have with Your Adult Children

The Iceberg You Don't See: The Marketing System for Financial Advisors Co-authored with Parthiv Shah

18 Wealth Lessons That Will Transform Your Thinking: Why Prosperity Seldom Taps You on the Shoulder After Years of Anti-Wealth Programming

Join the movement, get your free subscription to
The Equal Opportunity Critic Times by scanning
the QR code below or visiting EOCritic.com
and hitting the subscribe button.

The Equal Opportunity Critic Times is written by
Rodger Friedman, the Equal Opportunity Critic,
without the aid of artificial intelligence (AI).

Contents

Welcome to my book

Its Purpose

To provoke thought and discussion, to share my personal conservative philosophy, and the occasional rant. To make you aware of important events and stories you may have missed. To make sure your eyes are wide open. To memorialize much of the insanity we see from our media and our nation's leaders. To remind those who pay attention that our liberties and way of life are not to be taken for granted.

America is failing at succeeding

For the record, I categorically deny that I have, had, will, might, may, can, could, potentially have had, presumably might have, or may in the future will have access to classified documents.

QUESTION: According to the Federal Reserve Bank website, the *Fed* employs over 400 economists with a wide range of expertise.[1] So why is America acting like a drunken teenager who stole mom's credit card and has gone on a spending spree? The federal deficit reportedly stands at over $34 trillion and continues to grow as liberal members of Congress know no bounds in their ability to spend taxpayers' money. At what point does fiscal responsibility take over and a concerted effort to rein in federal spending is achieved?

PREFACE

During much of 2022, I found myself emailing friends and family numerous articles that I felt needed to be shared for no other reason than I felt they were indicative of the dangerous path this country has begun traveling. One Sunday morning, while sipping a steaming cup of mocha java from my favorite mug, I started writing an email to a small group of friends and family that summarized all the lunacy I had read during the week. I purposely kept it to one page and thought a once-weekly rant from me was quite sufficient. My goal was to share the two or three stories that got my attention and under my skin. With so much irrationality around me, I could not remain quiet. Little did I know I was at a turning point.

That idea birthed *The Sunday Memo.* It was November 2022. Soon, I realized that the weekly craziness could not be contained in one page and found that about 1,500 words each week were sufficient to get my points and opinions across. My messages—their trademark—was that they were frank, uncensored, and blunt with no sugar added and no apologies. They were raw, and if I pissed somebody off, so be it. They could unsubscribe from my weekly rant at any time. Oddly enough, few unsubscribed. After writing forty-seven *Sunday Memo*s, I felt they could be aggregated. My memos were meant to provide an ongoing chronicle of the lunacy and madness around us, how America is teetering on the edge of a cliff, and what might be done to right its course.

This book is peppered with discussions of headlines from a variety of media outlets and presents both facts and opinions. The facts are gathered from numerous sources, with attribution; the opinions are my own. Consider this book a wide-ranging conversation that showcases our country's repudiation of the values that made it great and features what many are saying about its decline. We have become a polarized yet fragile nation. We are shouting at each other and not listening. We as Americans must take to heart that we are one people, and never forget that **freedom is fragile**.

While Americans argue about transgender athletics, school bathrooms, the removal of urinals, and mandated tampon machines in boys' bathrooms, China rapidly expands its blue-water navy. While we allow men in college sororities and parade them on the cover of *Sports Illustrated* swimsuit issues, Russia, Iran, and North Korea become ever more dangerous world players. As a nation, our priorities have been misplaced.

**Our eyes are wide shut.
We are spending major time on minor things.**

While I don't present myself as a wise old sage, I have long passed the springtime of my life and am headed for life's winter. But I've paid close attention along the way. I've learned a lot, and I have things to say. I expect that some of what I say will keep you up at night but consider that a bonus since thoughtful Americans appear to be in short supply. We need all we can get.

This is not my first rodeo or my first book. In fact, I have written six books over the last ten years. Should you wonder how I kept busy over the last few decades, I manage retirement wealth. That has provided me with a front-row seat on how money moves about and how people behave when it comes to personal responsibility and providing for their futures without a paycheck.

This book is not for the timid American. We are all familiar with the sign found in many buildings: "In case of emergency, break glass." Well,

America is at a break-glass moment. As a society, I believe we have taken a wrong turn and it is up to us to get back on the right path.

Many will label me a *hard-core conservative*—somewhere between Newt Gingrich, Larry Kudlow, Mike Rowe, and Genghis Kahn. And yes, I have ruffled more than a few feathers. You will find me opinionated and direct—yet I speak from the heart. I have strong convictions, among them is the rule of law. I believe in funding the police, not defunding them.

Someone once said that politics is a nasty business, so there is no cute or soft way to get my message across. I stand my ground, supported by facts, truth, and my view of what is moral and what is not. I fully support conservative causes with my money and deeds. One subscriber called me an *equal opportunity critic*—I guess that's as good a description as I can hope for.

I am a proponent of a secure and strong border, intelligent and decisive immigration policies, a strong dollar, deregulation, curtailment of federal spending, energy independence, states' rights, a small federal government, low inflation, a balanced budget, and low taxes. If this disturbs or antagonizes you, best you put this book down now and read the *Washington Post* or the *New York Times*. You'll feel more at home there. In fact, why not move to Chicago, Minneapolis, San Francisco, Portland, Seattle, or New York City?

Since this book aggregates many months of *The Sunday Memo*, there are familiar references to past events and headlines, as well as questions of how a set of circumstances will play out. I purposely did not edit the content to allow for final resolutions of legislative actions, court decisions, and such. That is meant to place you, the reader, in the historical action play by play, month by month.

The material for this book is sourced from far and wide, along with my own ideas, insights, philosophy, and opinions. I have tried my best to provide accurate information for who said what to which media outlet and when. Any mistakes in attribution are mine.

I am the son of a hard-working entrepreneur. I believe in working for a living, not standing in line, or lying on the couch awaiting the next federal handout. If one wishes cradle-to-grave security, best they be housed in a prison, Cuba, North Korea, Venezuela, or Iran. It's called work for a reason, which also happens to be the title of a wonderful book by personal development pit bull, Larry Winget.

Understand that *I am an equal opportunity critic.* I call out local, state, and federal governmental actors for their harebrained schemes, intellectual dishonesty, stupidity, and socialist leanings. Whether a council member, Congressman, Chairwoman, Senator, or President, I am quick to call out foolishness and ill-conceived plans disguised as well-considered policy. You will quickly find that I don't pull punches. I call out well-deserved pinheads at every level of government. Ethically challenged politicians exist in both political parties, although I find the Democrats are far ahead of Republicans in this regard. Nevertheless, I single them out for poorly considered statements, ridiculous legislative bills, and idiotic comments in their speeches.

My opinions are not limited to government officials. Today's media is culpable for disseminating stories that can hardly be called news and is largely made up of crap that is not fit to print. The media's obsession with everything *trans* is evident on the front page of nearly every online media outlet on a daily basis. Stories of humans behaving poorly ooze out of every page and paint a story of a democracy out of control. Telling fake news from real news has become an art and science.

An email I received from a *Sunday Memo* subscriber sums up my current view of media's non-objectivity very well. It reads as follows:

The liberal media in America has become increasingly biased and partisan in its coverage of the news. This has resulted in a lack of objectivity, with news outlets catering to their respective political agendas instead of reporting the facts. This has often led to biased and incomplete reporting, as well as the spread of misinformation. The media's focus on sensationalism and divisive topics has also detracted from its ability to inform the public on the important issues of the day. The liberal media has become a megaphone for certain political ideologies, drowning out the voices of those who may disagree. This has resulted in a polarized media environment that has further divided the nation.

I couldn't agree more.

And lest I forget, I find great quotes both entertaining and instructive. In the pages that follow, you will see quotes by noted authorities, historical figures, famous folks, captains of industry, and others. I am a great believer that wise words, whatever their source, should never be forgotten, belittled, or lost in the fray. Whether these words were said by Thomas Jefferson, Warren Buffett, Paul McCartney, or Alexander Hamilton, I leave no great quote on the curb. I have found that great ideas often come from reading history and staying informed, something more Americans might try.

In a letter to Jonathan Jackson in 1780, John Adams expressed the founding fathers' fear of tribalism—something they felt could ultimately destroy liberty. He wrote the following:

There is nothing that I dread so much as a division of the republic into two great parties, each arranged under its leader, and concerting measures in opposition to each other. This, in my humble apprehension, is to be dreaded as the greatest political evil under our Constitution."

With that warning, I had fun writing this book and I hope you have some fun reading it. My sister called it the perfect bathroom book for the thinking conservative. I agree. But don't miss the lessons. There are plenty of them in these pages.

So then, let's get on with it…

Introduction

A wave of fear and nausea washed over me. My blood pressure spiked; my heart felt like it was beating out of my chest as I looked down at my sweaty palms. Was I experiencing a *crisis in faith*? Faith that my government was flying off the rails, and gone off the deep end? Was this great experiment—our enduring Constitutional Republic, coming to an end? Surely American politicians know better and took an oath to support and defend the Constitution. Were their oaths of office just hollow words without weight or meaning?

It was a Saturday morning in the fall; I sat in the comfy reading nook off my kitchen, sun shining in through the window, steaming coffee by my side, MacBook on my lap, reading through the day's headlines. I routinely scanned *Reuters*, *Fox*, *Newsmax*, the *Times,* and a few others for good measure. Headline after headline convinced me I was experiencing life in a Bizarro world, where up was down and right was wrong. Each headline describing actions by Congress or the President that smacked of socialism, unfairness, and outright violations of our country's most sacred American Foundation, the American Constitution. Vladimir Lenin's words came back to me: "*The goal of socialism is communism.*" I felt like my world had been turned upside down. Was I in Soviet America? I wanted to throw up.

The reality is, I have little faith that the electorate will vote the current crop of liberal Democrats out of office as long they continue to promise more and bigger chickens for every pot, courtesy of the Federal Treasury.

Yet as I write this, my concern is that some will pigeonhole me as out of touch with *today's America*. Some will agree with my words. Others won't. But I'm writing this because I think I have some important perspectives to share with the world. My opinions might be significantly different than yours, or we might see eye to eye. As hard as it is to understand a different perspective, Jack Canfield, the co-creator and author of *Chicken Soup for the Soul*, explained it to me this way: "Suppose you are on the beach, and someone tosses you a multi-colored striped beach ball. From their perspective, they see white, red, and blue stripes. Yet as you catch it, you see green, yellow, and orange stripes. You both see different colors, and you are both right in what you see."

Likewise, both sides of the political spectrum have important points. It is not my intent to demonize Democrats in general—I have friends and family members who vote Democrat. I see Democrats as very compassionate with a desire to help many people. Yet I see Republicans holding to the concept of personal responsibility and smaller government—something I personally believe to be the foundation of our great country.

As a country, we are not listening to each other. Look at the daily media. We are blaming, ripping, roasting, shredding, and bad-mouthing each other.

Headlines show their bias like sharp teeth on a Doberman. Gone is the civility that used to characterize the democratic process. Members of Congress vilify each other daily in the press. I fear we have grown immune to it. It is *our new normal*, and it's not a good thing.

Consider me a Mossberg twelve-guage shotgun. Strong medicine, and for good reason. My best guess is that one-third of readers will be perturbed, bewildered, and put off reading this book. Another one-third will praise it, recommend it to friends, family, and colleagues, and even go so far as to write glowing blurbs on Amazon pages. And one-third of you will recoil in horror. You will shudder and sob that

I had the nerve to write this, and you will tell me to seek psychiatric counseling. This book was written for the middle third, the third that matters.

I worry that our politicians are voting to provide every conceivable benefit, normally reserved for American citizens, to people who entered this country illegally and broke our laws. I fear the eventual economic collapse under a centrally, poorly planned economy, a fast-track to national bankruptcy. After all, someone has to pay for these benefits (i.e., entitlements). I can't be the only one worried that our politicians are endorsing defunding police departments across the nation and ignoring increased crime statistics. I can't be the only one who understands economics and sees the immense harm that unrestrained federal spending is having on our economy. I can't be the only one concerned that the *open-border party* seeks never-ending Democratic one-party rule.

I could go on and on. I won't. Suffice it to say that what you tolerate you get more of. We tolerate Social Democrats elected to high office who hate America. They seek to change it, make it more like Venezuela, Cuba, or the Soviet Union of old. They speak of equality for all. The American dream rests upon equal opportunity, not equality of outcome, enforced by the machinery of a massive government-run bureaucracy. If I work my ass off and you sit at home playing video games and watching TikTok videos, you are not entitled to my outcomes that I worked for. You had the opportunity to work your ass off, just as I did. The difference in our outcomes has EVERYTHING to do with our behavior.

Socialist-leaning Progressive Democrats seek to guarantee affordable housing for all, free universal healthcare, and a family-sustaining wage. I would point them to all the failed Socialist nations of the world and the misery created by governments that attempted this. They represent Marxism 2.0. The indoctrination is real, the changes are real, and our altered laws are stunning. They push the cradle-to-grave benevolence of a central government that will tell you where to work, how much you will earn, where you can live, and what kitchen appliances you are allowed to use. The government will provide healthcare for all—bad healthcare. The government will attempt to provide education for all, and it will fail—kind of like "no child left behind." Plenty were left behind, but as a sound bite it worked like a charm. If this doesn't scare you, you are not paying attention.

What we are looking at is an all-out assault by misguided, Marxist-leaning politicians intent on tearing down our country and our way of life.

Ideological intolerance has become both an art form and a contact sport among the ultra-left Squad members of Congress.

The current administration is erasing our Constitution. We are no longer a nation of laws that benefit all Americans. New laws and regulations passed by unelected bureaucrats who treat people unequally provide money and benefits to certain groups and not others. Equal protection under the law—sound familiar? It's the cornerstone of the Fourteenth Amendment of the Constitution below:

All persons born or naturalized in the United States, and subject to the jurisdiction thereof, are citizens of the United States and of the State wherein they reside. No State shall make or enforce any law which shall abridge the privileges or immunities of citizens of the United States; nor shall any State deprive any person of life, liberty, or property, without due process of law; *nor deny to any person within its jurisdiction the equal protection of the laws.*

Farmers and ranchers receiving assistance based on skin color? Not in America, you say. Think again. The Biden Administration has kicked the Fourteenth Amendment in the teeth while the mainstream media turns a blind eye. Thank heavens the courts gave that a swift sword.

Think it's not happening here? You haven't been paying attention. Look at the headlines, and you may weep for your America—the

America you grew up in, the America where you stood for the flag, repeated the *Pledge of Allegiance* in school, and respected and supported the military. That's the America I grew up in—the America that was respected around the world. It's not today's America where we are ridiculed around the globe and laughed at while our ineffectual leaders take their eyes off the ball and spend major time on minor things.

What we are seeing is the erasing of America by delusional, inauthentic Progressives bent on installing Marxism 2.0 in our country. **As long as they control the narrative, America is at risk.** While we squabble about who is allowed in which bathroom, the southern border has all but been erased. Millions of illegal aliens are disappearing into the bowels of this country, aided by the federal government. It is true, and it is shameful. While we argue about biological men competing against women in sports, fentanyl by the tractor-trailer load is turning our communities into cesspools.

In the following pages, I highlight how our media spins story after story. I provide some insight, commentary, or rant, depending on how despicable or illogical I find the subject. My goal here is to arm you with an awareness you may lack. You might have a sense of all the goings-on, but as we attend to our lives, our families, and our business, we tend to miss important items.

I am here to fill in some of the blanks so you can make more informed decisions the next time you go to vote, which I hope is IN PERSON with PHOTO ID and a VERIFIED SIGNATURE. And no, I don't think that is racist. I think it shows common sense, something we, as a nation, are sorely lacking.

I would urge you to be uncompromising in your stance against woke ideology and indoctrination, the continued assaults on our freedoms and liberties, and socialist ideology when you see them in your communities. Decide with your wallet where you will spend your hard-earned money. Frequent establishments run by patriots, not gutless Socialists hell-bent on upending our Constitutional Democracy. **Cancel the cancel culture** by joining together with other like-minded Conservatives. Get out and vote. This needs to end now.

Who will safeguard our republic if not us?

MEMO # 1

Politicians parade some facts and hide others.

The media had their own agenda

While China's laser-focused path to Asian Pacific hegemony gets scarier each year, our governments spend more time fighting each other than helping solve the nation's problems, and much of the media tells us that everything is peachy. Needless to say, my faith in media objectivity is at a lifetime low.

Be careful which media you allow into your mind. It seems that the media's favorite pastime is reporting on what Hollywood actors and athletes think of world events. Who cares what LeBron James thinks of Twitter and Elon Musk?

Who cares what a Kardashian thinks of being skinny, and why does it find its way onto the front page? Kid Rock blasting Oprah? Really? More and more, media news outlets report opinions of their owners, not factual news.

Civility is dead

As troubling as this is, I have witnessed civility among government officials go right out the window. The name-calling, the insinuations, the outright lies, the ridicule, and the obfuscations have reached unheard-of levels. Excuse me, but I thought members of Congress were supposed to be upstanding citizens and act in a dignified fashion. Gone are the days when members of Congress said, "I yield to the gentleman from South Carolina." Now we hear, "Mr. Speaker, I turn the floor over to that ass from South Carolina." Perhaps Congress can learn civility from the Hells Angels?

Politicians parade some facts and hide others

Accusations by politicians conveniently omit salient facts. Yes, the COVID-19 pandemic ushered in a new reality for the world's oil and gas industry.

According to Rystad Energy,[2] the five integrated *supermajors*—ExxonMobil, BP, Shell, Chevron, and Total—posted a combined record loss of $76 billion in 2020. Yet our president, along with Senators Warren and Sanders, only focus on one particular earnings period, which was excellent by any measure.

The president proclaimed, "Exxon made more money than God," and then said we should impose a windfall tax on them. Reading the June 11, 2022 edition of *Forbes Magazine*,[3] I was struck by the difference in Exxon's net earnings and Apple's. The companies' reported earnings were approximately $5.5 billion for Exxon and $25 billion for Apple. Guess Apple made a smidge more than Exxon! And by the way, it seems Exxon paid $2.8 billion in taxes for the quarter, so I guess they are good corporate tax-paying citizens. Cherry-picking facts seems to be the Administration's superpower.

There is no freedom from want

It's no secret. **I want a Porsche 911**. Prices I see are $100,000 for brand-new models. I'm intelligent enough to understand I can't just manifest my new Porsche, sitting under an olive tree and thinking it into existence, full tank of gas and keys sitting on the front seat. *But*

I do want the car. Unfortunately, there is no freedom in America that says I can or will get the car of my dreams. In other words, *there is no freedom from want.*

I suppose all those who agreed to repay loans for attending college want the government to repay those loans. I suppose everyone who committed a felony by sneaking into this country without permission wants the federal government to pay for a four-year college degree, to provide free healthcare and other assorted items like free housing and transportation, and to provide them permanent legal residency. They all want these things, and hopefully, they won't get them on my dime. We all want things that we are not entitled to. As for the Porsche, I understand I am not entitled to it so I will work and save and buy it myself. That's the American way.

Safeguarding our republic

Today's progressive liberal socialists do not support the idea of, or existence of personal liberties, preferring instead a super-sized nanny state, that will clothe, shelter, educate you, feed you, and hold you accountable to a one-party state from cradle to grave. They seek to dictate the appliances you have in your kitchen and laundry room, the car in your garage, and how you are permitted to mow your lawn.

NOTABLE AND QUOTABLE

**Today is already the tomorrow which the
bad economist yesterday urged us to ignore.**

–Hazlitt, Henry. *Economics in One Lesson*—Harper and Bros.

**When a government betrays the people by amassing
too much power and becoming tyrannical, the people
have no choice but to exercise their original right
of self-defense to fight the government.**

–Alexander Hamilton, Founding Father,
First Secretary of the U.S. Treasury

MEMO # 2

Am I the deplorable the President refers to?

Am I the deplorable the president refers to?

I remember watching President Biden give a speech on one of his many whistle-stops to drum up support for Democratic candidates. He used highly inflammatory terms to describe Republicans and all those who threaten his progressive, liberal agenda. The language he used made my blood run cold—deplorables, traitors to America, semi-fascists, and threats to democracy. I have never ever considered myself a "deplorable."

Yet, I am a "deplorable" because I do not agree with his radical Progressive Socialist agenda. I pay my taxes on time, I am gainfully employed, I stand for the national anthem, I have never been arrested, I give generously to important causes and charities, and I hold the door open for old ladies (and young ones too). *But in President Biden's mind, I am not the kind of American he wants here.* Unbelievable!

Midterms come and gone–badly

As I write this, I am reminded, painfully so, that this week the American people have spoken. The 2022 mid-term elections are now in the rearview mirror, although final results may still take a while. Through full and fair elections, many ex-politicians will now seek careers at Facebook, The *New York Times*, the ACLU, and progressive companies that will embrace hiring such distinguished minds that contributed so much to our way of life. Phooey!

My friend Lee is a world-renowned business strategist, speaker, and best-selling author—she is a woman who is not easily rattled. Yet recently, Lee sounded a chilling alarm that focused on the potential for disruptions and mass demonstrations, even riots after Tuesday's mid-term elections. She addressed the fact that the media is no longer an objective source of news and facts and that we as a society derive the majority of news from Facebook, Google, and dozens more big tech companies.

Big tech liberal Progressives

Big tech companies, whose names we all know so well, overwhelmingly supported progressive liberal Democratic candidates in the last election cycle. That makes me question America's sanity. There have been dozens of articles detailing how the large tech companies of our age are overwhelmingly supporting Democratic candidates over Republican candidates. Seems many of the liberal students who graduated from our nation's liberal colleges got jobs at liberal companies where they feel comfortable expressing their liberal views. That's a virtuous circle if ever I saw one.

A ribbon for ninth place

Ever wonder what happens to kids when they grow up and enter the workplace without a head full of confidence and self-esteem?

Well, they need constant reinforcement that they are doing okay. Doubt this? Read on.

I remember when my kids were little in Maryland. The enlightened school we sent them to was all about equality and everyone being a winner— show up and win a trophy! Then I thought back to my own public-school experience in lower Manhattan. I never received a ribbon for ninth place for perfect attendance, which brings me to a pet peeve.

Our society has become hooked on "atta-boy" and "atta-girl" attitudes like a coke addict hooked on their afternoon high. The MRI technician, the dry cleaner, the print shop, the tire store, the dentist's office, glutten-free pizzeria—they all send me surveys that ask me to rate my experience. I got nine of them in a week. Unfortunately for them, I never fill them out. If they want to know how they are doing, they should ask their parents!

Semi-fascist Ayn Rand reader?

I have never considered myself a semi-fascist. I've read my favorite book, Ayn Rand's *Atlas Shrugged* over a dozen times. But the president and his faithful followers see us as economic illiterates and fools. I'm a great believer in creating economic prosperity. I believe that entrepreneurs are America's greatest hope for a bright future. They sense opportunities, start businesses, hire employees, pay taxes, and create more for all.

I'm sorry but I do not believe that a bloated government is America's brightest hope for the future.

I believe in the rule of law and support local law enforcement whenever I can.

I continually provide free meals and my books at no cost to local police officers. I gave away my books freely. It's my way of saying thank you. I wanted to remind them that their current careers—protecting and serving others—do not preclude them from achieving a financially successful future.

I have had conversations with two seven-figure earners who trace their early careers to law enforcement. One was an Iowa prison guard, and the other was a Dayton, Ohio police officer. Now they are super successful entrepreneurs who help other budding entrepreneurs. I call this a virtuous circle.

Faith in the media? Have they earned it?

One other note on the media's favorite pastime—the reporting of the absurd. Why on earth would a major national media outlet run a story telling of a senior American Air Force official insisting that the flight path of our jets was not intentionally mimicking the shape of a man's penis? Do you think the Russians were up in arms as our Air Force pilots were figuratively giving them the finger, or other body part?

You just have to shake your head at stuff like that. You're probably wondering why the media would write and print that story. And yes, some idiot in that organization green-lighted the story. Needless to say, my faith in the media is at a lifetime low, principally because they have not earned it.

NOTABLE AND QUOTABLE

A legislative act contrary to the Constitution is not law.

–John Marshall, Chief Justice of the Supreme Court

**We must learn to live together as brothers
or we will perish together as fools**

–Martin Luther King Jr.

MEMO # 3

Have no doubt—stupidity is alive and well in Washington, D.C.

I spent a weekend in New York City attending a musical memorial for my oldest best friend, Steve. We were classmates in third grade, fourth, fifth, well, you get the idea. He passed away at the all-too-young age of sixty-five. We stayed in touch for all those years, saw each other occasionally, and enjoyed many great conversations. He was a professional audio engineer and musician, and an incredible, caring human being. We began guitar lessons at the same time, somewhere around fifth grade. He excelled; I couldn't even tune my guitar. He had an excellent ear; I had an earful of cauliflower that couldn't distinguish a G chord from an E chord.

While in Manhattan, I walked around my old neighborhood and spent an hour remembering all the great times. What was new were all the electric bikes zooming back and forth, ignoring stop signs and traffic lights. It is literally the new danger you have to watch for. Troubling as well were all the millennials walking down the street, heads buried in their phones and not looking where they were going. And I'm not talking about a few. I'm talking hundreds. Evidently, I annoyed three women who thought it was my responsibility *to move out of their way!* Seems if you don't subscribe to the millennials' style of living you are persona non grata.

And in case you thought I wouldn't get around to it, America's *inner idiot* was on full display this past week as candidates who favor law and order, a strong southern border, and fiscal conservatism did not fare as well as I had hoped. Remarkably, Madonna is not Treasury Secretary and Jimmy Kimmel isn't the Secretary of Defense.

My friend Lee says I should never be surprised at the stupidity of the American people. Unfortunately, she is spot on. Can this situation be fixed? Perhaps. But I do have my doubts because *we are the jokers who voted these jokers into power.*

Poor parenting disrupts an otherwise delightful dinner

But let me share with you what did surprise me during that weekend. I went to dinner with another great old friend, John. John is a professional musician who used to jam with Steve. Since I am the tone-deaf friend, I didn't participate in those sessions. Anyway, John and I are at dinner at a beautiful Indian restaurant on the Upper East Side. Seated a few tables away is a family with two kids around four years old.

These **brats** are banging their silverware on their plates, making all sorts of racket. They keep this up for over thirty minutes. Everyone in the room is looking at them. The parents are oblivious. I ask the server to bring the manager over so I can have a word. I am told that the manager is on break—*at the height of the dinner hour*—and there is no one who can speak to the parents.

I remember when my kids were little. If they made a nuisance of themselves, we picked them up and took them outside so we would not annoy all the other patrons. We wanted to teach our kids a lesson that that sort of behavior wouldn't be tolerated. Guess times have changed. On display for everyone to see was a prime example of bad parenting. Welcome to *the new America.* I would have liked to haul off that father by his neck, but *I am now enlightened,* so I think it but don't do it . . .

Now, some insanity for you to chew on

Governor Doug Ducey of Arizona has taken an admirable, incredible, and common-sense action to protect his border at a time of madness when President Biden has failed miserably. Ducey has ordered shipping containers by the thousands to be stacked at the border to physically block the path of illegals entering our country. I think this smacks of genius. The containers are low-cost and plentiful. And guess what the response is from the federal government. The Bureau of Reclamation said the unauthorized placement of the containers constitutes a violation of federal law and is considered trespassing. They have filed a lawsuit against the governor. Have no doubt—stupidity is alive and well in Washington, D.C.

Oh, and here's my fantasy: lawsuits back and forth quickly. The case goes to the Supreme Court, and the Arizona governor is found to be preserving our country's safety and security. President Biden is found to be culpable and negligent in protecting the borders of the United States and ordered to complete the wall that President Trump began. BAM!

NOTABLE AND QUOTABLE

I think myself that we have more machinery of government than is necessary, too many parasites living on the labor of the industrious . . . A government big enough to give you everything you want, is a government big enough to take away everything that you have . . . As government grows, liberty decreases . . . The two enemies of the people are criminals and government, so let us tie the second down with the chains of the Constitution so the second will not become the legalized version of the first."

—Thomas Jefferson, Founding Father,
Third President of the United States

MEMO # 4

Watching the two billionaires
speak is frankly riveting

I remember reading an intriguing discussion on the effects of government COVID-19 policies on the economy. It appeared in the October 2022 *Imprimis*[4] update from Hillsdale College, and it was a real page-turner! The author, Jeffrey A. Tucker, traces government actions from March 15, 2020, to the present, including the edicts, the lockdowns, the tradeoffs, the executive orders, and the policies that threw the economy into a tailspin.

He spoke of Americans getting used to the idea of the Federal Treasury depositing money into everyone's savings and checking accounts—and of course, that money tended to be spent, not hoarded. Amazon had a field day. The journey to 9 percent inflation had begun.

Santa Claus will be providing one and all a healthy dose of Christmas inflation—driven by the shortage and fast-increasing prices of **diesel fuel**. The price of diesel directly affects inflation since it increases the cost of inputs for goods sold. That drives up costs for industry, and in turn, those costs are passed on to the consumer. Inflation ain't gone by a long shot.

Federal imbeciles, state, and county too

The United States currently has little or no manufacturing for almost any component needed to produce solar energy. China, which can produce solar components less expensively, controls more than 80 percent of the supply chain. But politicians and energy executives say that if the United States becomes more reliant on solar power, then depending on China for equipment could present a security risk. Oh really? Gee! Who knew?

And good riddance to Montgomery County, Maryland—my home for more than twenty-five years. News sources reported that my county introduced a new book list that included LGBTQ books complete with illustrations and words such as Intersex and "Drag Queen" to young kids. I find this vile. Good riddance to Montgomery County.

If you live in Baltimore, take note. The Maryland legislature is hell-bent on providing more and more benefits to illegal aliens. Hearings are scheduled on bills to allow illegal aliens to apply for and receive occupational and professional licenses. I may be a somewhat simple fellow, but it appears to me that Maryland is trying to manipulate and undermine our immigration laws in order to keep illegal aliens in the country. 'Nuff said.

Random thought

If you have children, are you worried about the America they will inherit?

A chance encounter

No, I didn't know there was a movie titled, you guessed it, *A Chance Encounter*. A couple years back, I had a chance encounter with Dean Martin's Rolls Royce. I walked out of a hotel in Cleveland, Ohio, and BAM! There she was. I love that stunning piece of automotive craftsmanship, and *I love Dean* (along with

Frank Sinatra and Tony Bennett). As I marveled at this automobile, I thought I couldn't let this moment go by without capturing it. I had a friend take several photos of me posing with the iconic car and then had one of the photos made into a personalized greeting card. I still use those pictures today. TIP: Next time you have an encounter that rocks your world, capture it, use it in your life, and share it with others.

A billionaire's point of view

Elon Musk intrigues me. He possesses an extraordinary mind, one that thinks to ask questions no one else asks. He routinely works one hundred-hour weeks. He works, he sleeps, he works, and he sleeps. Small wonder why graduates from some of America's top engineering schools overwhelmingly want to work at Tesla or SpaceX. Consider this: Musk is one of the richest persons in the world and yet spent three years living in his factories, sleeping under his desk, on a couch, or in a tent he installed on the roof. Who does that? A CEO who wants his employees to know *he is all in.*

You may want to watch a fascinating interview between Ron Baron, CEO of Baron Funds, and Elon Musk at the 29th Baron Funds Investment Conference. Musk is the *Iron Man* of our age. You'll find the interview at Baronfunds.com[5] in the section about shareholder meetings at Lincoln Center. **Watching the two billionaires** speak frankly is riveting. *My judgment creates the future, one capable, I think, of creating a multi-planetary space-faring civilization,* Musk said.

NOTABLE AND QUOTABLE

Sure, there are dishonest men in local government. But there are dishonest men in national government too.

—President Richard Nixon

Just because you don't like the person or the organization, doesn't mean that the facts they present are false. Don't shoot the messenger!

—Rodger Friedman

MEMO # 5

I'm not big on non-citizens, felons, and illegal aliens voting

It is written, and perhaps true, that on the final day of the Constitutional Convention of 1787, crowds of Americans stood outside Independence Hall awaiting results of what type of government was crafted within the walls of that great building. History tells us that Ben Franklin was asked, "What do we have, a republic or a monarchy?" Franklin replied, "A republic, if you can keep it." A republic is a form of government where the people—the citizens—hold power but elect representatives to exercise that power.

In December 2021, the New York City Council passed a measure that would allow 800,000 noncitizens to vote in New York City's local elections. A State Supreme Court judge in Staten Island put an end to this abuse of power by the City Council and struck down the law. I'm not big on non-citizens, felons, and illegal aliens voting in elections. Not to be outdone by their liberal neighbors to the north, Washington, D.C. is pushing for illegal immigrants to have voting rights. In a twelve-to-one vote, the D.C. Council passed the resolution. Should Mayor Muriel Bowser sign the bill into law, Texas Senator Ted Cruz will immediately introduce a Congressional Review Act resolution to withhold federal funding to D.C.

New England muttonheads

Pipeline development hasn't kept pace with demand. According to ISO New England (an independent, non-profit Regional Transmission Organization headquartered in Holyoke, Massachusetts), natural gas accounts for 38 percent of the nation's electricity and close to 53 percent in New England. Yet the region is forced to rely on tankers carrying condensed liquefied natural gas (LNG) shipped to the Everett Terminal in Boston Harbor. Many of these gigantic ships travel from Algeria and Trinidad to supply New England with LNG.

This method of moving gas that is chilled to minus 260 degrees for transport is much more expensive than, say, a pipeline from the colossal Marcellus Shale gas field in western Pennsylvania. Oh, and lest we forget, the Marcellus has an astounding 410 trillion cubic feet of gas, enough to supply the United States' gas needs for more than a century.

So, a reasonable person (he, she, it, they, or them) might ask, why not build a honking big-ass pipeline to move the gas less than 400 miles from where it's produced to where it is needed? Well, the answer is NIMBY—not in my back yard. For years, New England politicians have rejected numerous pipeline development plans that would bring cheap, abundant supplies of natural gas to one of every two residents. The result is natural gas that's three to six times more expensive than in Texas, Louisiana, and most of the United States. And the wonderful citizens of New England keep electing these muttonhead politicians to represent them. Hey, you get what you vote for.

Who knew?

Seems there is a brouhaha over Taylor Swift's private jet emissions. Really? Call out the National Guard!

Ivy League Princeton University—you know, the $79,000-per-year bastion of higher learning in New Jersey—released its spring

2023 course list. Highlights include a course titled Black + Queer in Leather: Black Leather/BDSM Material Culture. Yet another reason to send kids to State U for one-tenth the cost.

The United Kingdom (you know, those folks across the pond) just increased the windfall oil and gas tax to a whopping 75 percent. Seems they have taken a page from the Norway/Venezuela playbook. If Mr. Biden and his friends taxed me 75 percent, I would just stay home and drink hot cocoa.

Random thoughts

My ideas for the best new occupations for Hunter Biden:

- Director at a county drug rehab agency
- Barista at Starbucks
- Director of pharmaceutical safety at a major drug company
- Nanny for your grandkids
- Ethics teacher at Yale University

Thank you, Joe Biden

Thank you, Joe Biden, for making America the laughing stock of the world, for runaway inflation, for doubling home mortgage interest rates, for draining the Strategic Petroleum Reserve for political purposes, for the botched and deadly Afghanistan military withdrawal, for skyrocketing energy prices, for your detestable Progressive agenda, for halting construction of a secure border wall, for calling me a semi-fascist, for damaging the U.S. economy, for your incredible hypocrisy, for politicizing the Justice Department and the FBI, for your disaster at our southern border, for your anti-energy regulatory policies, for permitting millions of illegal aliens to enter the country, and oh, for selecting a vice president who is beyond incompetent. Need I go on?

Attention, millennials

- Yoga pants are not proper workplace attire.
- You don't receive a trophy at swimming practice for putting your face in the water.
- You are entitled to nothing other than the air you breathe—everything else you work for.
- The world is not here to entertain you.
- There are no high fives for showing up.
- No one cares to see a photo of your lunch on Twitter, Instagram, or TikTok.

And finally, I think it's fitting that the *New York Post* proclaimed, "Millennials need to put away the juice boxes and grow up."[6]

NOTABLE AND QUOTABLE

Our country is blessed with extraordinary energy abundance, these energy exports will create countless jobs for our people and provide true energy security.

—President Donald Trump

MEMO # 6

Government insanity—state and local

It's illegal:

- to drive blindfolded in Alabama
- to be drunk while in a bar in Alaska
- to keep alligators in bathtubs in Arkansas
- to use a leaf blower to dry your butt in West Virginia

For those with a keen mind, can you figure out which "law" I made up?

Government insanity—state and local

Uncut bagels are normally tax-exempt in **New York**, but a bagel that has been "altered" in any way by toasting or adding cream cheese, for example, is suddenly considered taxable and automatically jumps in price by eight cents. Who else but ignorant politicians would enact this law?

California Governor Newsom still can't put forth a plan to get California's estimated 150,000 homeless residents off the streets.

California stands proud with its "housing first" model—an approach to provide the homeless with government-subsidized housing, while not necessitating any drug treatment or psychiatric care. On a lighter side, it appears the governor got a haircut and some serious hair gel.

It's a real shame, mixed with a bit of the absurd that the Arizona Legislature voted to provide in-state college tuition breaks to non-citizens. Okay. So, a kid from out of state—say West Virginia—will pay higher tuition than an illegal alien who crossed the border, evaded customs and border police, and is a criminal in the eyes of the government.

OPM, the U.S. Office of Personnel Management, is the chief human resources agency of the federal government. It's responsible for the policies affecting millions of federal workers.

On the other hand, the **OCM**, the Office of Cannabis Management, is a relatively new agency in New York State. Honestly, I'm not making this up. This agency is responsible for granting retail licenses to those who want to sell recreational cannabis. Interestingly, the NY State Legislature (majority Democrat) promised that the first licenses would go to convicted felons—those who were convicted of marijuana-related offenses before recreational use was legalized. Personally, I think the whole New York State Legislature is stoned off their collective asses.

Your annoying federal government at work

You would have to be living under a rock to be unaware of the massive student loan bailout proposed by the Biden Administration. The idea of forgiving up to $20,000 of student loan debt because *life is hard* is beyond anything I believe to be rational. And so it is not lost on you, the term "forgive" is not exactly accurate. You see, what the president has in mind is to *transfer* the obligation from the individuals who of their own free will entered into a loan arrangement for the express purpose of receiving a college education to federal taxpayers who have either paid off their loans, never took out loans or did not attend college. Whether this is legal or not I have no idea. No sooner had the Supreme Court struck down Biden's plan—literally hours later, the Biden Administration came up with PLAN B to forgive these loans. Evidently, the administration is unaware of the term "checks and balances."

What the president has in mind is for all the voters whose loans are cancelled to be so grateful they vote him and his cronies back in office for another four years.

And so it's not lost on you, while this is going on, the president's plan to release 180 million barrels of oil from America's Strategic Petroleum Reserve has me smacking my head against the wall repeatedly. I firmly believe he is doing this for political purposes while weakening our readiness for true national emergencies or war.

The now-famous investigation into the Dobbs leak at the U.S. Supreme Court that began in early May 2022 may never be resolved. Evidently the Supreme Court Marshal knows only one investigative speed—*slow*. It's time to bring in the detectives from TV's *Law & Order*. They wrap up an investigation in a little under an hour, and the *perp* always lands in jail.

What does this even mean?

- Pundits littering Twitter (Do we need a trash can?)

- A Twitter storm (Umbrella and raincoat anyone?)

- Leftists cause the *Twitterverse* to implode (should we call the bomb squad?)

- Disparaging barbs cluttering Facebook and Twitter (no clue what do here)

(I assume this is where barbs, litter, condescension, and annoying language went to congregate.)

Random noticeables (sentences that do exist but shouldn't)

Democratic Party strategist Adam Parkhomenko tweeted, *Lauren Boebert has not tweeted in 34 hours.* This begs the question: is there a *tweet clock* no one told me about? How do I get one—if I cared?

Years ago, I drew a fence around Facebook, Twitter, Snapchat, Instagram, TikTok, Buzznet, Bebo, and a host of other social media platforms and refused to participate in any of them. It seems I have not suffered undue harm from that decision and remain productive and engaged. The fact that millennials think I'm crazy does not bother me in the least.

Chew on this

Here are some provocative and interesting questions. If our society has agreed that there should be age restrictions on a variety of behaviors, such as drinking, smoking, entering into a contract, joining the military, and driving, why are there no rules laid out for social media use by the youngsters? Unless you're an idiot, you must have noticed that our children are glued to their devices six hours a day. Tell me how this is healthy! "Go out and play, Johnny" used to mean going OUTSIDE and hitting a ball or riding a bicycle. Now it's sitting on a stoop, glued to Instagram and Twitter, and watching TikTok and YouTube videos of dogs on treadmills and monkeys doing ballet.

Several countries in Europe, among them Switzerland, Ireland, and Germany have imposed a sixteen-year-old age restriction that must be verified. Perhaps the USA can learn something from them. I'm just sayin' . . .

I've read that many of the original laws with respect to social media were created to protect kids from data collection. The problem is that the laws were written before the creation of Facebook, Twitter, Instagram, and Snapchat.

Spotlight on the unobvious

I shudder just speaking these three letters together—AOC. Ugh! I feel like I need a shower. It seems that Ms. Cortez, commonly known by her initials, AOC, is always upset with Senator Ted Cruz of Texas. Not one to draw immediate conclusions, I decided to review each of their résumés and get a true sense of their experience and accomplishments. I think it's enlightening, and I want to share it with you.

Senator Ted Cruz

- Princeton undergrad
- Harvard Law School
- Clerked for U.S. Supreme Court Chief Justice William Rehnquist
- Domestic policy advisor to President George W. Bush
- Conservative Republican
- Attorney at the Justice Department
- Attorney at the Federal Trade Commission
- Solicitor General of Texas
- Argued eight cases before the U.S. Supreme Court
- Private practice attorney
- Long-term marriage
- Father of two daughters
- Two-term United States Senator

AOC

- Youngest woman elected to U.S. Congress
- Progressive Social Democrat

- Declared Socialist

- Substantial social media presence (Twitter)

- Boston University undergrad with a double major (international relations and economics)

- Waitress

- Bartender

- Appeared in a dance video

- Organizer and activist—Bernie Sanders Campaign for President

- According to Center for Effective Lawmaking[7] (a joint project of Vanderbilt University and the University of Virginia), she is ***among the least effective members of Congress***

Guess who draws more media attention? And yes, you may draw your own conclusions. Oh, by the way, it seems Ms. Cortez was not always paying attention in class. If you watch her questioning folks during Congressional hearings, you will immediately recognize that she doesn't have a grasp of basic economics. Perhaps she cut class to dance in the bar that later hired her as a waitress and bartender.

Partisan injustice

This is unbelievable. I am not a fan of Brooklyn federal judges. Seems that Urooj Rahman, a former practicing attorney, was sentenced to fifteen months in jail for lobbing a Molotov cocktail at a police car during the George Floyd protests in May 2020. U.S. District Judge Brian Cogan ordered former attorney Rahman to pony up $30,000 in restitution to the City.

Rahman unapologetically told reporters, "The only way they hear us is through violence."

Someone throws a **firebomb** and gets fifteen months in jail and a

$30,000 fine? This was a gravely serious crime that calls for a harsh sentence. When someone throws a firebomb, I believe the intent is to kill someone. If you want to destroy property, you can do that with a hammer. What ever happened to "throw the book at them" or "lock 'em up and throw away the key"? Crimes should have consequences. Severe crimes should have severe consequences. Period.

Is this former attorney (yes, they took away her license to practice law and her mother is now weeping at all the money she wasted on her daughter's law school education) now a threat to society? Must Starbucks baristas be extra careful not to mess up her order for a double latté venti with two shots of vanilla, extra foam, extra hot for fear of being fire-bombed by this lunatic?

Thank you, Joe Biden

Biden continues to harp on *gas station owners* to lower their prices at the pump. As a lifelong student of economics, it is apparent to me that the mechanisms by which global oil prices are set are extremely complex, and placing blame on big oil as well as the owner of a Chevron station in Sawyersville is misplaced. The extra two cents per gallon charged by my Sawyersville station owner was a conscious decision so he and his wife could afford to set aside $200 per month to fund each of his three kids' college educations so they wouldn't have to work thirteen hours a day at the family gas station.

Yes, our politicians actually said this

U.S. Secretary of Transportation Pete Buttigieg believes a rail worker strike 'would not be good' for the economy.

Washington Examiner, November 22nd, 2022[8]

I've now been to 57 states, with one left to go.

—Barack Obama at a campaign event in Beaverton,
Oregon, May 9, 2008

I love California; I practically grew up in Phoenix.

—Dan Quayle

I think that gay marriage is something that should be between a man and a woman".

—Arnold Schwarzenegger, California Governor

You know, there's a uh, during World War II, uh, you know, where Roosevelt came up with a thing uh, that uh, you know, was totally different than a, than the, the, it's called, he called it the, you know, the World War II, he had the war—the War Production Board.

—Joe Biden, rambling and struggling for words during an
April 2020 CNN interview about the coronavirus response.[9]

Random thoughts

Let's talk about civility or the lack of it in the halls of Congress and in the media. It seems that our elected officials never tire of **mocking** each other. Mocking? Really? I think the last time I *mocked* somebody was in seventh grade. And then there are liberal pundits **gloating** and denigrating those who do not subscribe to their points of view. Remembering back, I definitely *gloated to my friends* when I bought my first ten-speed bicycle with money I saved working at my dad's laundry. Yes, puberty and that blue bike definitely occurred in the same year.

Elon Musk should buy MSNBC and fire everyone.

Do you enjoy criticizing others? Do you like mocking them, trashing them, ripping them, blaming them, bashing them? Then maybe you should run for Congress. You'd fit right in!

NOTABLE AND QUOTABLE

**Things are more like they are now
than they have ever been.**

—President Gerald Ford

MEMO # 7

Say it ain't woke

It's illegal:

- to cross the street while walking on your hands in Connecticut
- to carry an ice cream cone in your back pocket on Sundays in Georgia
- to reincarnate without permission in China (my favorite!)
- to shake hands while underwater in an Ohio municipal pool

Your federal tax dollars hard at work

Media reports that during the month of December 2022, over 232,000 illegals crossed our southern border. This number should be zero. What part of this do you not understand, Mr. Biden?

I am not opposed to a portion of my federal income taxes paying for Medicare and Medicaid. I understand that these are important safety nets for a big portion of the American population. What I find reprehensible is, that my tax dollars are being diverted to pay healthcare expenses for felons that crossed our border in the middle of the night and took up residence here. If it were up to me, I would redirect those tax dollars to the purchase of bus tickets to take them back from whence they came.

Likewise, I have a real problem with my tax dollars being spent on:

- Swedish massages for rabbits: $387,000
- Teaching mountain lions to ride a treadmill: $856,000
- Synchronized swimming for sea monkeys: $307,524
- Tweeting at terrorists: $3 million
- Funding kids dressing like fruits and vegetables: $5 million
- Government-funded ice cream: $1.2 million
- (Source: *CNS News*, Curtis Kalin, "Top 20 Worst Ways the Government Wasted Your Tax Dollars")

It doesn't take a genius to see that our elected Congresspeople are inept and waste our tax dollars. Given a choice, I would like my tax dollars to be spent on hiring and training additional law enforcement, Navy SEALs, and Army Special Forces. AND I want to tape their pictures on my refrigerator—kind of like adopting an elephant in Africa or sponsoring an orphan in Zimbabwe. Oh, and a picture of the bus full of illegal aliens on their way back across our southern border—that would be cool. I would love directing my taxes to these worthy goals.

Say it ain't woke

In addition to permeating elementary, high school, and higher education, the woke society has taken root and infiltrated corporate America. Hundreds of public companies go out of their way to inform the public through their advertising that they abide by inclusive policies, have diversity standards, and provide segregated bathrooms for every type of creature on God's planet. (Restrooms for non-binary non-humans are down the hall, first door on your left.)

You need do nothing more than Google your favorite online media outlet to see countless stories that defend corporate diversity, inclusion, left-wing groups, transgender youth, taxpayer-funded gender reassignment surgery, student loan forgiveness, and every woke sentiment. I have never seen a more vocal minority shout at the top of their lungs and capture such outsized media attention. It appears easy when liberal media organizations grant them a front-page soapbox while burying opposing points of view on the bottom of page thirty-seven. I have become suspicious of nearly every online article dealing with politics and politicians.

To this point, after watching the documentary "*The Trump I Know*" I came away with an intense feeling that the overwhelming majority of negative press coverage of Donald Trump has been fabricated, is inaccurate, pulled out of context, unfounded and paraded as gospel by mainstream media and hateful Marxists intolerant of the opinions other than their own.

That brings us to what the media are deliberately not saying. It seems they have gone out of their way to report little in the way of being patriotic, achievement-oriented, taking personal responsibility and becoming a productive member of society, an entrepreneur, or a responsible citizen.

Our vice president is mad as hell

First, I want you to understand that the last time I saw *The Onion* newspaper was in a metal vending machine above a subway station in Washington, D.C., about ten years ago. As I was heading to lunch alone and had nothing to read, I picked up a copy. To say this was one of the strangest papers I have ever read is an understatement. Yet when I saw an article detailing the Veep's desperate work environment it made me laugh.

The article made the outrageous claim that our esteemed vice president of the United States was losing her healthcare benefits because she was only working part-time and did not qualify as a full-time employee. Worse yet, she probably didn't qualify for a match on her

401(k). Perhaps Ms. Harris should apply for a teaching position in the Chicago public school system. I hear they have excellent benefits!

The sad state of higher education

I have a *Defies Logic Meter* that has served me well for many years. I look at something and say, "That defies logic!" I've always wondered why colleges offer inane courses that students sign up for and attend, and then the parents pay for them. And worse yet, these courses count toward the credits necessary for a college diploma. Makes you wonder if hard-working parents are even aware of the courses their children sign up for.

What's your opinion on the following classes?

- Tree climbing (Cornell University)
- Lady Gaga and the sociology of fame (University of South Carolina)
- How to watch television (Montclair State University)
- The art of walking (Centre College)
- The Game of Thrones (University of Virginia)
- The physics of Star Trek (Santa Clara University)
- The history of surfing (University of California, Santa Barbara)

Hey Sherlock. Check the undergrad course catalogs. But then again, I would question the decision-making ability of any college student who is paying their own way and would fork out $900 to $1,600 for one of these frivolous courses. Draw your own conclusions. Perhaps required college classes such as the ones below would provide the younger generation with more valuable skillsets. These classes represent real-world experiences that most if not all college grads will be faced with—better they have some idea of how to put useful knowledge on their side:

1. How to prepare for job interviews
2. Signing a lease—what you need to know
3. When should I begin saving for retirement?
4. Basic financial planning
5. The elements of a legal contract
6. Dressing for success
7. How to be productive
8. How to set goals 101
9. The art of car buying
10. Having a strategy for your career
11. Understanding basic taxation
12. Entrepreneurship
13. Failure 101
14. Decision making
15. Goal setting and personal development (advanced)
16. Why be a millionaire?
17. Giving back

Random thoughts

Elon Musk's neuroscience startup Neuralink is expected to give a progress report on its brain-implant technology. Were I to have a voice in the selection process, clearly Joe Biden should receive the first experimental implant . . . just sayin'.

The esteemed Janet Yellen, Secretary of the Treasury, is now blaming Americans for record-high inflation. Yes, this is truly a Teflon administration where everything is someone else's fault, and NO FAULT lies with the current administration.

Remarkable! I have yet to see the folks at Team Biden take responsibility for anything.

And lest you forget, there shall be NO mooning in the Hellenic Republic (the official name of Greece). It considers mooning an act of disrespect and provocation. The country has zero tolerance for mooning, and offenders can be arrested or made to do time.

November 2022 inflation-fighting Black Friday sales smashed all records as stores marked down prices to what they were when Mr. Biden took office.

What is transitory inflation? It's similar to regular inflation but with 20 percent more lies.

There is a silver lining to the story that Mike Lindell says he'll run for RNC Chair . . . he promised all Republican House and Senate members a new My Pillow for the low, low price of $19.95 (plus shipping and handling).

News you have absolutely no idea what to do with

It seems *The New York Times* is grappling with journalists not being happy in La La Left Land. It appears they were heading for a walk-out—1,000 of them. If we're lucky, they will walk out and never come back.

I confess, I have never heard of a porn-bot. Seems the Chinese government may (or may not) be responsible for swamping Twitter with these little critters in an attempt to block protest videos. These little *bots* may include pornographic images and the like. What I find fascinating is that this was discovered by researchers at the **Stanford Internet Observatory**.[10] I find three things remarkable about this.

First, that the Chinese government may be resorting to blocking Internet sites and searches in furtherance of its polices. I thought this was reserved for paradise places such as Iran and Venezuela.

Second, that there is actually such a thing as a porn-bot. Who knew? Is it like a little robot with boobs that talk dirty?

Third, not to sound like a broken record, but is there such a thing as the Stanford Internet Observatory, and do they have telescopes like real observatories and offer daily tours to fifth graders? Do they report on monster asteroids hurtling toward Earth? Are we on the verge of being smashed to atoms? Does NASA rely on the Stanford folks?

Well, we are still here, so the world-ending asteroid did not hit us. Maybe Taco Bell should have taken advantage of all the end-of-the-world hoopla and run an end-of-world fifty-cent taco sale.

Putting lipstick on a felon

Dozens of media outlets reported that The Deputy Assistant of the Office of Spent Fuel and Waste Disposition at the Department of Energy's Office of Nuclear Energy was arrested after video evidence of he/him/her/it stealing a Vera Bradley suitcase at the baggage carousel at a Minneapolis airport. Sam Brinton, a strapping, bald, six-foot, lipstick-wearing, high-heeled LGBTQ activist and nuclear engineer who fancies himself/herself/itself non-binary, was relieved of his duties at the Energy Department following the felony theft charge. What could make a mother prouder?

Spreading good cheer

You heard it here first—the Beatles will NOT be touring next year. I'm told that being a white male in the San Francisco government has become somewhat challenging. A colleague shared a *Newsmax* article (November 23, 2022) that discussed concerns about racial equity and how one or more government employees were forced to reapply for their jobs because they are white males. This is definitely NOT the America I grew up in.

I'm happy to share with you that some of my closest, most interesting, and very colorful friends are doing very well. Included among them are: Dagney Taggart, John Galt, Hank Reardon, and Francisco D'Anconia. You see, each is a character in Ayn Rand's monumental 1957 novel *Atlas Shrugged* that I read each December. I always look forward to visiting them and reliving the epic struggles of those who refuse to give in. This book has had a unique influence on the way I think and how I view life.

So, we are clear on this: I don't do hashtags or tweets. I don't Insta anything. A number sign worked quite well on a typewriter keyboard for over one hundred years and in a tic-tac-toe game.

NOTABLE AND QUOTABLE

Democracy means that anyone can grow up to be president, and anyone who doesn't grow up can be vice president.

—Johnny Carson

We have a system that increasingly taxes work and subsidizes non-work.

—Milton Friedman

MEMO # 8

I plan to buy one of those newly vacated countries

Evidently, there is someone who calls himself 50 Cent. Don't ask. I haven't a clue why anyone would go around town calling themselves fifty cents, thirty-two cents, or some other sub-dollar amount. Were it me, I would change my name to *Hundred Dollar Bill.* It appears that this fellow is a famous rapper. Fine. Why else would there be a headline in the online *Radar* article proclaiming, "50 Cent Scores Small Victory in Penile Enhancement Fight after Judge Rules Lawsuit against MedSpa Can Move Forward."[11]

I guess this rapper's penis and his small victory are major Hollywood news. Must be a slow news day. I don't feel any further comments are necessary on this subject.

Hey, people change

I never liked David Letterman. When he did late night, I thought he was an ass. Now he is old, has a long beard, and hosts an interview show on Netflix. He dresses chic down—kinda like right out of the Orvis catalog with a $390 sweater and $400 work boots. He did a Green Lantern interview—that was kind of cool. They made pizza together. I watched him interview Ukraine President Zelensky in a 300-foot-deep subway station. I like David Letterman now. He is intelligent and thoughtful. Hey, people change.

Law and order . . . Friedman style

I received a special invitation from the Clerk of the Circuit Court. No, I'm not being arraigned. Seems they want me to be a juror. I pity the defendant. I'm from the *Andrew Friedman School of Law and Order*—"lock 'em up and throw away the key. Next!" Hey, they asked politely under threat of law. The least I can do is show up early with long pants, shined shoes, and an attitude.

I vividly remember when my dad owned the laundry near Times Square in New York City. I was working at loading and unloading the massive dry-cleaning machine that stood about ten feet behind the front counter and cash register when an oh-so-foolish-would-be robber came in with a switchblade and demanded all the cash in the register. My dad, along with Angelo, our muscle-bound, abs-as-hard-as-steel manager, chased him out of the store and down the street, armed with steel pipes. I learned that day that a steel pipe has more uses than carrying water from one place to another. I'll never forget the lesson I learned that day at Norton's Laundry & Dry Cleaning.

DACA/the Dreamers

The Dreamer issue is complicated—kids brought here by parents who broke our laws. In my opinion, they do not deserve government benefits that taxpayers pay for. I'm talking welfare, unemployment, and Medicaid. Do they get a free pass? Not on my watch.

All those able-bodied men and women should be given a choice. Leave, or join the military and serve this country for a period of four years. We believe in choice—Army, Air Force, Marines, Navy, or Coast Guard. Take your pick, kinda like Dunkin' Donuts. *Their only choice to remain here legally is to serve this country.* And if they receive an honorable discharge, give them a free ride to a four-year public university, they deserve it.

Now, here is the fine print. If they have been convicted of a felony, they are deported after their sentence is served. We don't want them here. It's a step in the right direction rather than granting amnesty with a stroke of a misguided Democrat's pen.

Remember, there are no simple solutions to complex problems. Chew on that . . .

A little progress, day by day

I am making progress on my on-again-off-again twelve-step program to wean myself off my addiction to media. If you give a damn, here are the steps in my self-designed program:

1. Identify the media outlets that I know are not good for me.

2. Work every day—think, do not click on their websites.

3. Understand that I'm really not missing anything important.

4. Realize that I have more time to do what's important to me.

5. Remember that I control what I put into my mind.

6. Allow me to enjoy the small victories each day.

7. Revel in the idea that they get none of my money.

8. Smile when I think of #7.

9. Examine other areas of my life where I can duplicate this strategy.

10. Lean on friends when I need a boost to get me through the day.

11. Make no mistake—media addiction is an addiction.

12. Steer my attention to more profitable areas of life.

While it's true that I am making great strides in reducing my media diet, I still review the *Wall Street Journal* online each morning. Hey! I'm a finance guy. Cut me a little slack.

Anyway, a Cheshire-cat-type of smile was seen on my face recently when it was disclosed that federal prosecutors and the SEC charged eight social media influencers over an alleged stock manipulation scheme that made more than $100 million. One of them said, "Well gee, I really don't work for a living, but I do have 50 million followers." Well, that's nice, but it doesn't give you a free ride to violate the law.

Yes, it's really a thing

I was scanning bagel websites in an attempt to send a chewy and delicious gift to some clients. Seems no one wants the customer to choose what is sent. They want to choose it for you. I would rather choose on my own, thank you. Still, while performing my bagel due diligence, I was surprised to see a gift pack that includes—wait for it—flagels. Well drop me off on Broadway at midnight and call me Zelda. What the hell is a flagel? Seems it was born in Brooklyn in the early '90s amidst clamoring for low carb bagels. Seems they squish a bagel (maybe they get Nana or Pop Pop to sit on it?) and call it low carb. Genius!

Unreal estate

A tale of two investors I know: one was fantastically successful through experience and careful study, and the other one saw folks get rich in real estate and decided he wanted that. He bypassed the learning process of the fantastically successful fellow. He just wanted the outcome. After years of compounding one mistake after another, he sold. He had no gains whatsoever to show for thousands of hours of busy work with no carefully designed strategy and exit point. Might make a good book though . . .

And let the hysteria begin

Title 42 came to a screeching end on December 21, 2022. It is the government order that permitted the expulsion of so-called asylum seekers on pandemic grounds. If you feel like illegal immigrants flooding our borders daily was a sight to behold, just wait. I estimate that by December 31, 2023, the entire populations of Mexico, Honduras, El Salvador, Colombia, Venezuela, Guatemala, and Nicaragua will be safely relocated in the United States. Shortly thereafter, I plan to buy one of the newly vacated countries, build a big-ass wall around the border, and live out the rest of my days. Thank you, Team Biden.

We all have free speech

Many Progressive Liberals I have met appear to have an aversion to thoughtfully communicating with people they don't agree with. While I might see the world through a different lens, I am not the braindead Conservative they think I am. If they took the time to study history, they may wish to re-evaluate their current belief systems and stop trying to shut down any conversation that makes them feel uncomfortable.

Yes, we all have strong convictions, but I am at least willing to listen to opposing sides if they are presented in a reasonable and sane manner, as opposed to a disingenuous person, in my face, with righteous indignation, yelling and foot stomping.

Shortage continues

It's come to my attention that there is a worldwide shortage of billionaires. We are down to a paltry 3,111. If anyone would like to step up, I'm sure the world would be happy to welcome you. Don't care if you're young or old, come from oil or microchips, born in Cambodia or Camden, New Jersey, or have three or more testicles.

Just make sure that when you're done livin' it up, you leave the bulk of your good fortune to worthy causes.

NOTABLE AND QUOTABLE

**The obscure we see eventually.
The completely obvious, it seems, takes longer.**

–Edward R. Murrow

MEMO # 9

Don't say you weren't warned

Politics—state, local, and bizarre

I read that the U.S. Senate voted to ban TikTok on government devices. I applaud their wisdom on this. It's a matter of national security, and I for one want my nation to be secure. However, the measure faces a doubtful future in becoming law. Why am I not surprised?

I fear the rise of Progressive Democratic Socialists. Where they to have their way, they would tear down every monument and statue that honors the founding of the country and those fearless patriots who put all at risk to secure life, liberty, freedom, and happiness.

I view these Progressives as today's *societal disease*, fighting to erase our borders, embracing critical race theory, denying parents' rights, indoctrinating our young, denying two sexes in favor of a laughable unlimited number, endangering kids by denying them bathrooms designed exclusively for boys or girls, encouraging transgenderism and sexual reassignment surgery (even for minors) at taxpayer costs, and the list goes on and on.

And let's not forget the lack of intellect in the New York State Legislature.

How could someone be busted by the police with over 20,000 fentanyl pills and be set free? Fair question. The good folks of New York City dutifully charged the fellow with first-degree criminal possession of a controlled substance and then freed him without any bail requirement. Should you doubt me, I invite you to Google the following article:

New York Post—November 13, 2022
Man Busted with 20,000 Fentanyl Pills Set Free: Police Sources [12]

It's the economy, stupid

One of the many stories I read during December of 2022 in the *Wall Street Journal* was a story by John McCormick which told of the latest polls that suggest that among Republicans, 83 percent expect the economy to worsen. Slightly more than half of Independents feel that way, while only 22 percent of Democrats do. I was struck by the enormous disparity between Republicans and Democrats—83 percent vs. 22 percent. *I like my reality shaken but not stirred.* May the senseless and delusional Democrats' 401(k) balances melt away like ice cubes on a warm summer day!

The rumor mill

I imagine that part of the indoctrination process to become a partner at Goldman Sachs is they tie you down and tattoo the likeness of Alan Greenspan on your ass cheek while forcing you to listen to Lady Gaga.

Slow day in the newsroom

I vehemently disagree with any media outlet that publishes this kind of crap:

The Washington Examiner, December 3, 2022

"Detransitioner [is that even a word?] Who Had Breasts Removed Says She Is Suing Doctors Who Approved Surgery."[13]

After reading this article, I felt this was not even borderline news. If it's a slow news day and the media has nothing of substance to report, they should just take the day off and say, "Hey, we got nuttin."

From rumor to fact: Kim Kardashian gets $200,000 **monthly** child support. The absurdity of this statement stands on its own and needs no further comment.

Okay, so an actress, Meghan Markle, marries a "royal," and now the entire country is talking about her *power* cashmere sweaters. I don't get it. Maybe they're all looking at her boobs.

Don't say you weren't warned

I believe AOC is hazardous to the United States of America.

Ms. Cortez embraces the idea that if an illegal alien can sneak into this country, they are entitled to all federal benefits, including but not limited to Medicare, Medicaid, retirement benefits, and food stamps. Her 2019 House Bill—H.R. 5071: A Just Society: The Embrace Act[14]—was the brainchild of the economics-impaired, and a Socialist who is looking to *erase our borders and bankrupt this country.* If the House ever passed such a bill, it would open the floodgates even wider to illegal entry into this country.

Thankfully, the bill went to committee and never went any further. Here's the first part of the bill: *To provide access to Federal public benefits for aliens, without regard to the immigration status of that alien, and for other purposes.* Then it described some of those benefits: *Any retirement, welfare, health, disability, public or assisted housing, postsecondary education, food assistance, unemployment benefit, or any other similar benefit for which payments or assistance are provided to an individual, household, or family eligibility unit by an agency of the United States or by appropriated funds of the United States.*

Assisting the socially and economically disadvantaged, regardless of their immigration status, and providing for environmental justice—whatever that is—are some of the newest and more elastic *go to phrases* for Social Democrats to increase the population's dependence on government handouts.

What is terrifying here is that Americans voted this genius into office.

A borderless country is not a country at all. It is chaos.

Oh, be still my heart

There's something comforting about sitting down with *The Objectivist Newsletter.* I was recently gifted a beautiful hardbound copy of the newsletters, Volumes 1–4, written and edited by Ayn Rand between 1962 and 1965. They are fascinating. The parallels drawn between what she wrote about in the 1960s and today's *ass-hat politics* are riveting. Were that not enough, they include a tremendous essay by a young Alan Greenspan (remember that Fed chief?) called "The Crisis over Berlin."

I have earmarked a couple of Rand's interesting essays to dive into:

- "Leading a Rational Life in an Irrational Society"
- "The Goal of My Writing"
- "How to Judge a Political Candidate"

Do surprises never end?

I read of a *cryptoverse* that encompasses many of the crypto world's coins and tokens. Interestingly, approximately 8,000—or 40 percent—of these "investments" are now dead coins, having been deactivated or delisted. Dead money, it would seem.

And mortgage rates have more than doubled in the Biden years. The Federal Reserve was forced to take severe action to rein in inflation after our esteemed Democratic leadership stabbed our economy in the heart with its economic policies. The sheer incompetence of Team Biden is beyond words.

40% of Students at Liberal Arts Colleges Now Identify as LGBTQ, Study Finds—Eric Utter,[15]*American Thinker*, December 19, 2022

This 40 percent statistic came from the Center for the Study of Partisanship and Ideology, a center-right think tank that researches partisanship in academic and scientific fields.

What I find remarkable here is that nationwide, according to a Gallup Poll, approximately 7 percent of the nation identifies as LBGTQ. Yet almost six times that number (40 percent) identify as LBGTQ at liberal arts colleges? What can I say other than their mothers might be surprised . . .

Notable and quotable

Those who expect to reap the blessings of freedom, must, like men, undergo the fatigue of supporting it."

–Thomas Paine, Founding Father

Crime is common. Logic is rare. Therefore, it is upon the logic rather than upon the crime that you should dwell.

– Sir Arthur Conan Doyle

MEMO # 10

President Trump's tax-returns-release what to whom?

Congressional math

What are the odds Congress Will Pass HR 2617?[16] The bill, a massive 4,155-page document, will be presented for a vote, the outcome of which is a massive spending sledgehammer to the economy. My question is, who on earth, or in Congress, will spend the time to read this monster document?

The many newspapers reporting on this event did such a great job of *not hiding the lead* that you scarcely had to read the articles. Now consider the following: the idea that our nation's laws are often passed without our elected legislators even reading them. *The fine print* is often crafted by Senate and House staffers who are unelected worker bees in Congressional offices.

Were I a congressman (okay–you can stop rolling on the floor now) and was given a 4,155-page document on Monday for which I had to cast a vote on Thursday, *the math becomes highly problematic.*

For example, Monday through Thursday–three days. Let's call it seventy-two hours. Now these folks are busy, so let's say they only get six hours of sleep each night. Let's also assume the following:

- They don't commute
- They don't eat dinner, lunch, or breakfast
- They don't read their kids a bedtime story
- They don't have any family time at all
- They don't go to the bathroom
- They don't brush their teeth
- They don't get dressed

Here's the math: Seventy-two hours minus eighteen hours (for sleep) leaves fifty-four hours to read the bill in its entirety. That's seventy-six point nine pages per hour for fifty-four hours. I'm a rather speedy reader, but I couldn't read seventy-seven pages per hour any more than I could out-dunk Shaq, outspend Elon Musk, or out-hit Mickey Mantle.

Outcome? We're screwed . . .

Release WHAT to WHOM?

Evidently, the good folks in Congress have voted to release President Trump's tax returns. Put aside for the moment how distasteful this whole affair is, and my question is this: *Release what to whom?*

If the committee proceedings and all "evidence" are printed in the Federal Register, I fear that the tax returns will be viewable by approximately seven billion people on the planet. Common sense tells me that the documents in question **should only be released** to the relevant investigative committees and no one else. Anything other than that should be viewed as *revenge of the Democrats.* Let's call a spade a spade. Oh, and by the way, any unauthorized leaks should result in imprisonment.

Random thoughts

Texting wasn't invented to improve anyone's driving.

So . . . I overheard my kid's Starbuck's order—*iced toasted vanilla oat milk shaken espresso.* I think it has something to do with coffee, buts it's probably cheaper at Walmart.

I wanted to make sure I shared this. I go to an unnamed pizzeria each week and get a customized salad they make perfectly. One day, the owner wasn't in, so I had to painstakingly explain to the young lady my *off-the-menu* order.

While giving her my order, I noticed a sous chef in the kitchen cutting carrots. I thought, gee, I'd like to add carrots to my salad. So, I asked, and with a straight face, the young woman replied that they don't have carrots. I then explained that she may want to tell that to the young chef who was busily cutting carrots six feet from her. She frowned and grudgingly added carrots to my order. Right there is a wonderful argument against a fifteen-dollar (or more) minimum wage. Best she be retrained or fired.

The folks in Washington

You've heard it before, and it's happening again as I write these words. The government will shut down in a couple of days if a **must-pass spending bill** is not passed. Gee, where have we heard that before? *I assure you that you do not know where I am going with this.*

As before, we are told that the government furloughs all *non-essential* personnel and tells them, "Hey, stay home, we can't pay you. Put your feet up, grab a latté, and watch reruns of *The Bachelor*. We'll call ya when it's okay to come back to the office."

Well, it occurs to me that Congresswoman Alexandria Ocasio-Cortez, or *Sandy* as her high school chums called her, may in fact be non-essential personnel since she has been named one of the least effective members of Congress. May I suggest that Ms. Sandy stay home, grab a latté, put her feet up, and enjoy season after season of *The Bachelor*? After all, it appears she really doesn't have anything more important to do.

Atlas be shrugging

The cat is out of the bag. I'm an *Atlas Shrugged* junkie. In my first book, *Forging Bonds of Steel* (on page nineteen) there's even a caricature of me sitting by the fireplace reading *Atlas Shrugged*. So, don't be surprised if you see references to Ayn Rand and her characters from time to time. They have proved to be some of my greatest advisors and friends for many years.

I've noticed an unmistakable hatred on the part of certain members of Congress (Elizabeth Warren, Chuck Schumer, AOC) to American industrialists and billionaires in particular. I'm drawn to the parallel from *Atlas Shrugged* where the most productive members of society were ostracized for their great achievement and singled out for ever harsher treatment under an avalanche of laws designed to curb their success. The fact that Ayn Rand foretold with such great accuracy the incredible absurdity taking place in today's government is nothing short of miraculous.

Hell, let's take ALL their money!!

Wake up, Colorado—it's your turn

Were you to drive from El Paso, Texas, to Denver, Colorado, be prepared for a 650-mile journey. That hasn't stopped the parade of illegal aliens descending on Denver. What's interesting is that once they get about 1,500 illegals descending on their city they scream "NO MAS"—we can't take any more. They should understand what places like El Paso are going through, as they attempt to deal with an onslaught of illegal aliens. I'm sure Denver will declare a state of emergency and ask Biden for federal funds. I suppose El Paso can invite the mayor of Denver to come vacation for a spell.

It seems the illegals opt for Democratic strongholds such as Colorado rather than risk their lives in Montana, Wyoming, or Tennessee where the welcome mats are noticeably absent and many a resident carries a firearm.

A lump of coal this winter?

Europe is *grudgingly* relying on coal this winter to light and heat their homes and factories. That is certainly difficult for EU politicians who rail against coal and fossil fuels while supporting windmills and solar panels. It seems their choices have become simple and binary. You can freeze and die, or you can live to fight another day. Your choice.

Much like the flawed thinking of many American politicians, Europe's flaw is their timing and approach to transitioning the continent to renewable energy sources too soon while being utterly dependent on the untrustworthy Russian regime AND closing dozens of coal-fired power plants over the last ten years.

Being a bright political science major from a minor state university, I could have advised the EU leaders that they should not, under any circumstances trust the Russian government not to weaponize their energy policies. But hey, nobody called me.

NOTABLE AND QUOTABLE

Those who desire to give up freedom in order to gain security will not have, nor do they deserve, either one.

—Benjamin Franklin

A double standard of ethics—a demand that some men practice what others do not have to practice— is morally indefensible.

—Ayn Rand –The Objectivist Newsletter,
Volume 1, number 5- May 1962

MEMO # 11

Some potato latkes with your crypto?

Not a crypto success story

As a general rule, I do not follow the never-ending media love affair with the Kardashians. Granted, they know how to sell stuff, get on the front page, and become rich. Good for them. However, when a headline about them rises in the financial media, I can't help but give it a short glimpse.

It seems that at some time or another, Kim got fined $250,000 and had to sign a three-year consent agreement with the SEC as a penalty for promoting a specific crypto coin to her followers/fans on social media.

The crypto coin lost 100 percent of its value, and while fans love Kim, her investment advice? Not so much. You see, she had failed to properly disclose that she was a paid endorser. Selling unregistered securities is frowned upon by the SEC. Had the SEC any balls, the fine should have been $5 million—at least that would have gotten her attention.

Some potato latkes with your crypto?

Splattered across the news was that FTX co-founder and former CEO, Sam Bankman-Fried posted a bond of an astounding $250 million and would be allowed to remain free and live in his parents' California home.

I suppose a conversation between Sam Bankman-Fried and his parents would go something like this:

Sam's Dad: So, my grown-up Sammy, the U.S. Attorney says you perpetrated a fraud of epic proportions. You know, if you had taken over the family business and worked hard, you could have a fleet of laundry delivery trucks by now, but no, dirty clothes weren't good enough for you! And what about this gigantic bail amount? How did you raise $250 million?

Sam: They're blowing things all out of proportion, Dad. Do you remember how I socked away my bar mitzvah money, birthday money from Aunt Sadie, and earnings from plowing driveways in the winter and cutting lawns in the summer? Well, it all adds up. Besides, I like working on a computer, not washing dirty underwear.

Sam's Dad: Hey, you watch it there. Those dirty clothes paid for your college!

Sam's Mom: Stop it, you two. Well, Sammy, I'm glad my little bubbala is home. Would you like stuffed cabbage along with the kasha varnishkes? I can make potato latkes too.

Sam: Mom, you know I hate kasha varnishkes! But I love your latkes!

Sam's Dad: That's some fancy home jail bracelet you got on your leg, son. How long do you have to wear it?

Sam: They're worried that I'll skip the country.

Sam's Mom: Well, they did drag your tushy back from the Bahamas!

Shout-out to Senator Rick Scott

On August 16, 2022, Senator Rick Scott (R-FL) released a letter[17] to American job seekers that warned them against applying for newly posted IRS jobs. The job openings are a result of the Biden Administration's focus on spending $80 billion to hire 87,000 new IRS agents and expand the reach of the IRS by leaps and bounds. I congratulate my senator on his moxie and give him a shout-out: Go Team!

Excerpt from Senator Rick Scott's letter:

It is important to understand that in the initial IRS job posting for these positions, which the agency has now taken down, the IRS made it very clear that one of the "major duties" of these new positions is to "be willing to use deadly force." We aren't talking about joining your local police force, or even the U.S. military–this is the federal agency charged with collecting taxes. The IRS is making it very clear that you not only need to be ready to audit and investigate your fellow hardworking Americans, your neighbors and friends, you need to be ready and, to use the IRS's words, willing, to kill them.

Inflation-raising pork, anyone?

The $1.7 trillion spending bill passed in the waning days of 2022 (so Congress could get home for Christmas) is a fiscal abomination. True to form, the president promptly signed it, and presto! It became the law of the land. All 4,000-odd pages that a huge portion of Congress never read included billions of pork and pet projects.

The omnibus budget bill includes $410 million for border security in Jordan, Lebanon, Egypt, Tunisia, and Oman. *But I could find nothing pertaining to border security for the southern border of the United States. Evidently, Congress is worried about other countries' borders but not our own.* There are also big increases for universal guaranteed income programs *with no work requirement.*

The bill includes a mind-boggling 7,200 earmarks. An earmark is defined as "funding for special projects that members of Congress compete for to help their state or district."

The bill includes contributions for LGBTQ Pride Centers, the designation of a federal building in San Francisco as the Speaker Nancy Pelosi Federal Building, $3.6 million for a Michelle Obama Trail in Georgia, and a host of other spending measures that make me question why I pay federal taxes at all. Oh yeah. If I don't, they'll throw me in jail and take all my stuff.

Try as I might, I find it almost impossible to wrap my brain around the fact that 535 members of Congress shoved 7,200 earmarks into this bill for an average of 13.5 earmarks each. Departing Republican member of Congress Richard Shelby of Alabama scored more than $650 million in earmarks from the bill. Not a bad retirement gift. It sure beats a gold watch and a boot out the door.

Customer disservice

I felt you, the reader deserved to understand the depths of poor customer service in the post-pandemic age and what Americans are having to put up with. I purchased a really nice, chocolate brown, leather, three-ring binder and scheduler from a leading time-management company. So far, so good. After two months, the metal spine that connects the leather binder to the rings broke loose and started swiveling left and right as I tried to write in it. Prognosis: not good.

I call them. "Oh," they say, "that happens sometimes due to a loosening of the screws in shipping." Mind you, I got an explanation—not taking responsibility or solving the problem. I assumed they were grommets, one micron thick, since I couldn't see them without an electron microscope. I said, "Can you replace it? I can't continue to use this poorly made product of yours."

Answer: "We can send you more screws, and you can fix it."

Well, okay then. I have to fix their product, which malfunctioned on my watch.

Ten days later (yes, ten days) I got a package of screws that were beyond small. Five folks tried to screw them in. Impossible. TOO small.

I called them again.

Yada, yada, yada.

They agreed to send a replacement of the exact binder I have.

Great!

After waiting twenty days, I call. "Where's my %&*$&#^^@ binder?"

"Oh, it appears that this binder has been discontinued," they said.

ME: So, you didn't call me or send an email or singing telegram to inform me of that?

THEM: Oh, we're sorry.

ME: Well, that solves nothing. I still have a broken binder and am no closer to solving this problem.

THEM: Okay, we have another similar binder, different color, we can send you.

ME: Okay. Thank you.

Nine days later I get a binder with small rings (I had large rings) that I can't use.

I call.

THEM: Well, it appears that the person you spoke with entered the order incorrectly.

ME: You think???

THEM: The replacement does not come with the large rings.

ME: Well, why didn't anyone ever say that?

THEM: We can sell you one in black with large rings, but that's an extra twenty-five dollars.

ME (on the verge of wringing their neck through the telephone line): Okay, here is my credit card number.

THEM: We will ship it right out.

ME: Thank you.

Nine days later, I receive a package with a personal development book and a coupon for ten dollars off. (Was this their subtle hint that I needed further personal development?)

No binder.

I call again.

THEM: Our records show that your binder was delivered yesterday.

ME: No, you sent me a book that I have already read—and I still don't have my binder.

THEM: Okay, sorry, must have been a mix-up. We will send your binder by overnight mail.

Seven days later, I still didn't have the overnight shipment.

I don't understand how these idiots are still in business. You might have noticed that the service we receive from those we do business with has declined measurably. Mediocre is the new standard. Exceptional service? Maybe once in a blue moon.

Death train

According to a recent report by U.S. Customs and Border Protection officials, a train heading into Nogales, Arizona from Mexico was caught transporting 762,000 fentanyl pills. China continues to manufacture the base chemicals for the drug and sell them to Mexican cartels. Should you believe that China is a friend of America, I ask you to open your eyes and become more informed.

Not California again!

I fail to understand how California, which was never a slave state in the history books I read is on the verge of passing new legislation that provides reparations to certain African Americans residing in the state. Forget for a moment that no one living in California has been a slave, and that no one living in California has ever owned a slave to the best of my knowledge. These folks are long dead and buried. But somehow the geniuses that run the state have concluded that taxpayers living in the Golden State are responsible for reparations in the billions. Perhaps this whole thing was meant as a diversion to take everyone's attention off all the other ongoing and massive failures of the state.

Face it, poor people—including African Americans and others—have it hard in California. An honest assessment of the causes would require the Golden State's political establishment to admit that its attempts to address enduring poverty have been a catastrophic failure for low-income Californians.

Instead, Californians got a state reparations commission that time-traveled to the nineteenth century and discovered that slavery is the real reason for enduring black poverty. To settle accounts, the commission has determined that California taxpayers owe each of their African American neighbors $223,000. Leave it to California to focus on everything other than what is right in front of them!

NOTABLE AND QUOTABLE

Bet ya didn't know that there is a severe shortage of guns and money at the IRS. But hey, don't worry, Biden is solving that problem.

—Rodger Friedman

The appropriation of public money always is perfectly lovely until someone is asked to pay the bill.

— Calvin Coolidge, President of the United States

MEMO # 12

A feat worthy of a Democratic Congress and Administration

Pipe down, Bernie

During the height of the 2022 Southwest Airlines Christmas meltdown, Senator Bernie Sanders took to the media, yelling that Southwest was preparing to lavish $428 million in dividends to their wealthy shareholders. Perhaps Sanders doesn't realize this is a company with over $6 billion in revenues. Southwest pays a skinny seventy-two-cent annual dividend, equating to a yield of 2.16 percent—not exactly a big dividend payer!

In a perfect world, perhaps the self-proclaimed Socialist might want to review facts before spouting anti-capitalist generalities. In fact, a vast amount of the publicly held company shares—about 72 percent—are held by institutions, not wealthy shareholders. What are these institutions? Among them are Vanguard, Fidelity, Black-rock, and T. Rowe Price mutual funds. Who owns a large swath of mutual funds? Well, the simple answer is a whole lot of folks with 401(k) plans, 403(b) plans, IRA accounts, and the like. BUYAH, Bernie! Why don't you shut up and retire to one of your three homes provided by a capitalist society that you seem to hate. Alternatively, you can retire to a tin hut in downtown Havana and surrender your American passport.

Los Angeles landlords get the shaft . . . again

The Los Angeles County Board of Supervisors is well-versed in denying property rights to city landlords. They voted to extend the Covid eviction moratoriums further, as many apartment renters came down with the flu. Perhaps the owners of these rental units can provide a written excuse to their mortgage companies asking for an extension?

In addition to the eviction prohibition for tenants claiming hardships due to respiratory illnesses and the flu, the prohibition supposedly extends to tenants causing nuisances and having unauthorized pets. The original expiration date of the eviction moratorium was scheduled to end on May 31, 2020, yet the Board of Supervisors has continually found reasons to extend it over and over again. Where else but in the Soviet Republic of Kalifornia?

Woe to LA landlords! They're probably wishing for some great tenants in Iowa who pay their rent on time and are a dream to work with.

Random thoughts and enlightenments

While reading Chernow's epic biography *Titan* in which he chronicles the life of John D. Rockefeller, I stopped—for here was a word I had never heard before. *Quarrelsomeness.* It seems to perfectly describe the prerequisite and sole qualification for a job in Congress.

I'm told that there is such a thing as an Oprah-approved astrologist. Who knew?

This brings to mind a slew of questions:

- Can Oprah-approved astrologers market that title in their advertising and business cards, and do they pay Oprah an annual fee?

- Can Oprah-approved astrologers charge more than non-approved astrologers?

- Are you guaranteed in writing a better "read" if your astrologer is Oprah-approved?

- How much does Oprah charge for her approval rating?

- Is Oprah worried about competition from *Consumer Reports*, *Good Housekeeping*, or *The Ladies Home Journal*?

Grown-up money

I heard an interesting term on Tillman Fertitta's show, *Billion Dollar Buyer*. He was schooling a young pair of entrepreneurs who had worked all year and had less than $3,000 to show for it. He told them, "*Ladies, it's time to earn some grown-up money.*"

If you have not read his book *Shut Up and Listen!*, it is a great read.

A feat worthy of a Democratic Congress and administration

Among the many accolades for what the Democratic Congress and president have achieved in 2022, none stands out more to me than the simultaneous meltdown of both the bond and stock markets.

The mid-1960s saw the Federal Reserve raise interest rates as it sought to cool the economy—kind of like what's happening today. The economy fell into a recession in 1969, which helped create negative returns for both stocks and bonds. But the Feds went all out in 2022 and created a perfect storm for the financial markets with bonds and stocks falling in the double digits. In fact, 2022 will go down in the books as the worst bond market in over forty years. Thanks, guys!

With a Republican majority, my fervent wish is that the House of Representatives will kick some Democrats' asses and return some semblance of sanity to the federal government and the budget process.

Government work shouldn't pay so well

It seems on her last workday of 2022, Nancy Pelosi issued a directive and signed off on eye-popping raises for Congressional staffers. The directive specifies that staffers may receive salaries up to $212,100 per year—quite a bit higher than the $174,000 paid to senators and congresspeople.

My perspective is that government work *should not pay so high*. Perhaps with lower wages for staffers, we might enjoy smaller government and see the end to legislative bills with 4,000-plus pages. Think about that for a moment. A 4,000-page bill is equivalent to reading the 1,168-page *Atlas Shrugged* four times in a row!

For those who argue that higher government wages will incentivize the best and brightest to seek government work, well, it hasn't worked out so well for the Senate and House. Look who we are stuck with!

Unanswerable questions

If most Americans don't share the Democratic Party's inbred devotion to higher taxes and a bigger federal government, why do they keep voting them into office?

Evidently, Sam Bankman-Fried, before being arrested on crypto fraud charges, gave $40 million to a Democratic Super PAC. Evidently, a kid who graduated from MIT can be a complete butthead, right? Another reason to lock his ass away and throw away the key.

Why don't all low-wage, fast-food workers move to Soviet Kalifornia and Elizabeth Warren's tax haven of Massachusetts so they can enjoy the highest minimum wage of fifteen to twenty dollars per hour?

UPDATE: The state of Kalifornia is preparing to increase the minimum hourly wage for fast food workers (only) to twenty dollars per hour.

Ethics Committee tight-lipped

Unlike the rest of Congress, the House Ethics Committee knows how to keep a secret. While the country waits on pins and needles to learn of the charges against Congresswoman Sandy Cortez (D-NY), we can have a little fun and guess why she is being investigated for House ethics violations. Might it be because the obtuse and least-effective member of Congress was caught in the act of:

- Inappropriate behavior in a mattress store in Queens, NY?

- Pickpocketing Nancy Pelosi's purse in the Congressional cloakroom?

- Breaking into Senator Ted Cruz's home and spray-painting his dog?

- Knocking off a liquor store in the Bronx?

Anyway, it will be fun to learn the truth and see what happens since Congress is now controlled by the Republican Party.

Welcome to the economic twilight zone

I'm amazed at how my local supermarket is thriving. I stand at the deli counter, I'm the only customer, and three employees are scurrying around behind the counter. Not one of them approaches me. They are doing everything else except serving the customer right in front of them. Perhaps a *shock collar* would help them remember that their primary job is to serve the customer. Perhaps the collars should be around the necks of the incompetent managers who trained them. Rather than focus on minimum wages rules, maybe the company should look at the maximum amount of money they are paying these incompetents.

A spoonful of Ayn Rand's *Atlas Shrugged*

I had a fantasy—no, not that kind. I fanaticized that Ayn Rand's John Galt character from *Atlas Shrugged* was real, and on a mission to drain the USA of all significant power players who are liberal or progressive Democrats and rob Congress of the jackasses *who are running and ruining our country*. In the book, John Galt drained the brains of America, robbing the country of the best and brightest industrialists, leaving only the moochers to run the country, drive the economy into the ground, and leave the largest cities dark without heat or electricity.

I dreamed that in a speech broadcast on all networks, my fantasy version of John Galt was heard saying this:

I have instituted a strike of weak minds. You ask where all your liberal Democrats have gone. I have taken them from you. You ask where all the handouts have gone. I have robbed you of the morons who provided them. You ask why the border wall is being built with all deliberate speed. I have cleared all the roadblocks and allowed for a fully functioning republic and a strong economy built on entrepreneurship. A strong border is paramount in this endeavor. Don't ask where your politicians are. They are not coming back. We have arranged for their resettlement to Venezuela, Cuba, North Korea, and Honduras. Let them enjoy a Marxist way of life and appreciate permanent banishment from America.

NOTABLE AND QUOTABLE

Ethics is knowing the difference between what you have a right to do and what is right to do.

—Potter Stewart—Associate Justice of the Supreme Court

MEMO # 13

EPA wants to control every puddle
and wet spot in the country

Do transgenders love Kalifornia cash?

Fox 13 Seattle reported in April 2022[18] that Palm Springs was set to give universal income to transgender, non-binary residents r*egardless of earnings* for a period of twenty-four months. The City Council voted unanimously in favor of the proposal. By the way, the mayor of Palm Springs is transgender.

Okay, so I'm not sure what the presence of or denial of testicles or ovaries qualifies you for taxpayer-funded monthly handouts. These local government idiots should be hauled off to a shantytown in Cuba and never allowed to sully our shores again.

Where it me on the council, I would vote to provide low-interest loans so these non-binary citizens (?) so they can attend trade schools, learn welding or plumbing, and be useful—not useless—tax-paying members of society and get off the public dole.

In November 2022, San Francisco voted to provide low-income transgender folks a guaranteed (taxpayer-supported) income of $1,200 per month for eighteen months. *Who needs to be on welfare anymore?* Just come out as a gender-non-specific-non-binary and Kalifornia throws cash on you.

Close the gates!

According to *The New York Times* March 21st, 2022 article by Frances Robles titled *Stay or Go? Cuban Entrepreneurs Divided on Where to Stake Futures* approximately 250,000 Cubans have migrated to the United States and been granted residency by the Obama Administration. Unbelievably, that represents about 2 percent of Cuba's population! Meanwhile, the progressive Social Democrat legislators are trying to make these folks feel at home by passing laws intended to make America a Socialist paradise like Cuba!

On Dancer, on Rudolf, hey Schumer, hey Warren, hey AOC, hey Watters, hey Jayapal, hey Omar, hey Raskin, hey Tlaib, hey Sanders—I will buy your one-way airline ticket to Havana 'cause that's the kinda guy I am. Get your butts on the plane.

Sanctuary cities go from bad to worse

Liberal orthodoxy is responsible for much of the carnage we see in our Sanctuary cities. Billions of dollars of damages from riots where police were ordered by city councils and mayors to stand down and allow the looting, rioting, firebombing, and destruction of property to proceed while calls to police went unanswered.

What we are witnessing is a cultural breakdown, culminating in a toxic America. Witness New York City's woke politicians removing statues of George Washington, Christopher Columbus, and Thomas Jefferson. This is disgraceful behavior on the part of elected city officials. Our society is hemorrhaging and may well end up on life support.

Only in Oregon

Beginning January 1, 2023, all Oregon governmental departments must abide by new terminology that describes illegal aliens. Henceforth, they MUST be referred to as non-citizens. Evidently, there have been numerous incidents where Venezuelan or Cuban illegals have been confused and misidentified as Klingons, Romulans, or Martians. Go figure . . .

Only in Kalifornia

Los Angeles animal control personnel granted permission to a young lady to keep a unicorn in her home, provided she abide by certain rules. I feel discriminated against since my previous state of domicile, Maryland, denied me a permit for a pet dragon.

I'm not kidding

The ex-president and ex-vice president of Guatemala have both been thrown in jail on fraud and conspiracy charges and sentenced to sixteen years in prison. Hey, why not give prison terms to members of Congress and the executive branch who flout the law?

Maybe America can learn a thing or two from the Guatemalan judiciary.

City ordinance—you cannot explode a nuclear bomb within the city limits.

Law on the books in Marlborough, Massachusetts—you may not detonate a nuclear device in the city. I guess they want you to drive out to the country and detonate it there?

I was recently introduced to a new method of acting disdainful to others: instead of paying attention, the "listener" instead chooses to scroll through their phone messages.

Doubling down on stupid

What do you bet that when Biden finally made it to the southern border he looked around and said, "I don't see any problem, do you?" I'm sure they vacuumed up all the illegals hours before Air Force One landed.

Dedham, Massachusetts—the only town in America whose library decided NOT to put up a Christmas tree. A *firestorm* ensued and ended in death threats. I kid you not.

"Let's Go, Brandon" still thinks Vice President Kamala Harris is the President. On multiple occasions, he let it slip on televised talks. Personally, my choice for president of the United States, in order is:

1. Donald Trump

2. Nikki Haley

3. Ron DeSantis

Biden's Environmental Protection Agency (EPA) is blatantly expanding its grip on every puddle and wet spot in the country. The EPA has issued new Clean Water Act regulations that will make it more difficult and expensive for people to build roads, bridges, and homes. The *hubbub* comes down to the definition of "Waters of the United States." (WOTUS) For decades that meant *navigable waters* such as rivers, lakes, and canals. But leave it to the EPA to expand the old definition and in doing so make an end run around

Congress. The new definitions are expanded to include mudflats, sandflats, wetlands, sloughs, prairie potholes, wet meadows, playa lakes, and natural ponds.

Shame on you, *Wall Street Journal*

After reading the article below, I felt that the *Wall Street Journal* had sunk to new lows. I find it strange *how the media reports* a story of a rapist and murderer being sentenced to death by a Missouri court and then that death sentence being carried out. On January 3, 2023, Amber McLaughlin's death was reported as "Missouri Executes Transgender Inmate, a First in the U.S."

In this case, the *Wall Street Journal*'s only angle was that the inmate was transgender and that she/it/they/them/it/whatever was the first in the United States. Shame on you, *Wall Street Journal*. I recommend you fire that editor and start reporting news for news' sake. Had the offender been a run-of-the-mill murderer and rapist, the newspaper would probably never have reported on it. My take? *The media is obsessed with everything trans—and it's time for them to get off the bandwagon.*

NOTABLE AND QUOTABLE

Long ago, any one deal wasn't going to change who paid for jet fuel for my plane.

—Sam Zell, real estate multi-billionaire

Marriage is nature's way of keeping us from fighting with strangers.

—Alan King, famous comedian

MEMO # 14

The energy barons are to blame—far from it

Hey media! Who cares?

The lesbian partner of the White House press secretary quit her job at CNN. That is *all over the media* simply because the press secretary is gay. If a heterosexual government worker's lover/spouse quit a job, it would be reported nowhere, and no one would give a damn.

Every story about Prince Harry published in the United States should come under the heading of "Why would I care?"

News reports tell us that classified documents were found in a Washington, D.C. Biden think tank. Mind you, I'm not certain exactly what that is, as I have rarely seen the president think. The media goes on to report that White House staff notified the National Archives, who then took possession of the documents. The stories were rather cut and dried; we found the documents and called for their removal.

Yet when classified documents were found at Trump's estate, the media went ballistic. Folks lit their hair on fire. Whoopi Goldberg drove her car off a cliff. Democrats screamed at the top of their lungs, and 4 million liberals cried foul. Hmm . . . two presidents . . . classified documents . . . two totally different outcomes.

**It will be a delight to see how this is played out
in Washington, the media, and the courts.**

Blame

Hey, baseball, move over. Blame has become America's new national pastime. *Big tech* has become the new de facto media with Facebook/Meta deciding whose posts they will delete and whose are allowed to pass through their liberal gates. In addition to big tech, giant news outlets routinely spin stories based on their politics. It seems practically impossible to read unbiased news since that does not seem to command as many eyeballs as salacious headlines that clearly blame someone or some group for something.

It might interest you to know that universities and colleges routinely restrict Conservative speakers from filling their auditoriums to speak on important subjects. Many are turned away or their events become circuses complete with protesting student groups who don't agree with the speaker's point of view.

Case in point: A conservative speaker event was abruptly canceled at the University of California, Davis in October 2022 after over one hundred protesters and counter protesters fought.

The *Associated Press* reported on October 26, 2022 that protesters wearing "Proud Boy" shirts and members of Antifa were among those involved in the brawl. During the same month, Penn State cancelled a speaking event due to threats of violence on campus.

Interestingly enough, it is not the Conservative groups who are protesting liberal speakers—it is the liberal and Socialist groups trying to prevent Conservative ideas from being expressed on their campuses. And the blame is squarely placed on the gathering of students attending the event, not on those who seek to disrupt the events and the speakers.

Whether you spend time with your phone, your iPad, a daily newspaper, or the 6:00 p.m. TV news, I'm certain you will see that *blame* is front and center in many stories. You have the editors of the media organizations to thank for that.

Sanitizing El Paso

It was nothing short of amazing. Days before the president flew to El Paso on January 8, 2023 for an *inspection* of the border, federal agents descended on the area with barrels of Clorox and literally disinfected the town. Garbage was hauled away, illegals were hauled away, tents in the immigrant camps were dismantled, churches were cleaned from top to bottom—and the president was presented with a pristine town that by all outward appearances was right out of Andy Griffith's Mayberry. Instead of seeing a border town failure of massive proportions, the *pres.* was treated to pageantry worthy of a Miss Universe pageant. I'm certain that Mr. Biden may have commented, "Looks good to me!"

If Barbados sues Dr. Strange, I sue Egypt

Benedict Cumberbatch, the actor who played Dr. Strange in Marvel movies, may be sued by the island nation of Barbados. Word has leaked out that his great-great-great-great grandparents owned slaves on the island, and because of his bloodline, he may be asked to pay reparations of over $1 million for the deeds of his ancestors. While discussions are in their early stages, it does appear that British media may have fabricated a large portion of the story. Nevertheless, it is very entertaining. A Marvel superhero is sued because of his ancestors' misdeeds. Maybe that could be a storyline for a future Marvel hit!

But while we are on the subject of misdeeds, I have a bone to pick with Egypt. Thousands of years ago, the land of Egypt enslaved my people. They were slaves for generations. I firmly believe that I, along with millions of my kin, are due a sizable sum from Egypt for the horrible treatment of my people all those generations ago.

Should Egypt provide a public apology, perhaps from the stage of the United Nations, and pay us in gold measured by our body weight, that would go a long way to ease the pain they inflicted on us. Of course, fat people would end up with more gold, but hey, they will need it for medical care down the road.

It's all about the Joneses

Some background—the Jones Act was enacted by Congress in 1920. The law requires any cargo that is shipped between U.S. ports to be carried by American-built, -crewed, -owned, and -flagged ships. In recent years, there have been many good reasons to abolish or change the law since it adds significant costs—especially energy costs—to numerous goods moved from one city to another.

The Cato Institute has been working on a project called the Jones Act Reform to help educate Americans and Congress on how this one-hundred-year-old law is no longer serving America's best interests.

What I find most interesting is that an update from the Cato Institute revealed that a Freedom of Information Act (FOIA) request has uncovered government Maritime Administration documents recommending to "charge *all past and present members of the Cato and Mercatus Institutes with treason.*"[19]

It seems Cato has hit a raw nerve. It will be interesting to see how this plays out. Stay tuned.

Oh, for the love of Henry

Henry Hub is not a person; it is a pipeline junction in Louisiana. It is *the place* where natural gas is priced in the United States. There is no shortage of media reports detailing how natural gas is much more expensive in California than in other parts of the country.

From time to time, parts of California experience huge jumps in the price of Henry Hub natural gas. Of course, Mr. Hair Gel Governor

Newsom tells us that the energy barons are to blame. Far from it. His state's efforts to heat their homes using mirrors and windmills have fallen far short since two-thirds of the state heats their homes with natural gas. SoCalGas (Southern California Gas Company) has warned its customers that they will likely see energy costs double. In fact, a dear friend in northern California told me that her natural gas bill skyrocketed from fifty-six dollars to over $400 monthly.

The problem is the pipelines—or lack of—allowing gas to flow into the state from places such as Texas, North Dakota, Montana, Pennsylvania, Ohio, and others. You see, the Unites States is up to its collective ass in gas. We have enough to supply our needs for a century—yes, that's one hundred years for you grade-school dropouts. Now follow this logic—Democrat-controlled Kalifornia placed a moratorium on new pipelines in an effort to wean themselves off of fossil fuels.

Hey, Gavin, how's that working out for ya? Can you spare some hair gel?

Renegade ideas

Do you speak English? has been labeled as a microaggression in some Texas hospitals.

Hey, if you want a microaggression, this Texas hospital's administrators all need to be fired. How's that for aggression?

NOTABLE AND QUOTABLE

You can always count on Americans to do the right thing—after they've tried everything else.

—Winston Churchill

MEMO # 15

We think it's good, but it might kill you

Illegals treated to budget-busting hotel stays

New York City Mayor Eric Adams is up to his neck in illegals. Can't say I'm sorry for him. I'm not. He and other mayors of sanctuary cities are finally getting a taste of what it's like to be on the front lines of the illegal alien crisis. Stories are emerging of New York City renting hundreds of hotel rooms for $300 plus per night to house the influx.

Newspaper reports tell of $500-a-night rooms, trashing of the hotels and sex in the stairwells. A disgrace that can be laid at the feet of the city government.

I applaud Texas, Florida, and Arizona governors for their steel-encased balls to send planeloads and busloads of illegals to D.C., Chicago, and New York City. They're giving these sanctuary cities a taste of what it's like to live with massive influxes of illegals—made possible by the Biden Administration.

In addition, I find it ironic that the mayors of these cities are now crying foul. They're calling their situations emergencies that are straining their resources—exactly what Florida, Texas, and Arizona have been saying for two years while their pleas have fallen on deaf ears in the Democrat-controlled White House and Senate. The liberal-controlled media that provided scarcely any coverage is now splashing it across the front pages.

If you were wondering whether he's a knucklehead—he is!

In my opinion, Hakeem Jeffries, the House minority leader, is a knucklehead. He was bent out of shape due to new House rules that Republicans had instituted to right the sinking House ship. As you read the comments below, ask yourself this: Are these rule changes bad, and are they something a reasonable person is apt to agree with?

Excerpt by Jack Hellner, *American Thinker*, January 13, 2023:[20]

Jeffries's concern is due to people who want America to be "great again"—or in other words, full of freedom and prosperity for all. *The headline at Breitbart read: "Minority Leader Jeffries: House GOP's 'Extreme MAGA' Agenda Will Undermine Well-Being of Americans."*

I would challenge Mr. Jeffries or anyone else who agrees with him to show how the following rule changes, or votes negotiated by the "extreme MAGA" Republicans, are endangering the welfare of the American citizenry:

1. *Requiring each bill to deal with a single subject instead of being loaded with irrelevant stuff. Proposed legislation should be a reasonable length and understandable. Seems rather uncontroversial, right?*

2. *Requiring seventy-two hours to read the bill before a vote. What a concept—learning what is in a bill before they vote. I bet Nancy Pelosi isn't a fan!*

If you don't want the fun to end, read related articles on the rule changes and how the media has reported them.

In case you forgot

Back in 2019 when Crazy Bernie Sanders was running for president, he implored voters in an interview on Vermont Public Radio not to discriminate against him because he's an old white guy. He went on to say, *We have got to look at candidates, you know, not by the color of their skin, not by their sexual orientation or their gender, and not by their age. I mean, I think we have got to try to move us toward a nondiscriminatory society, which looks at people based on their abilities, based on what they stand for.*[21]

Seems he was getting desperate that his Socialist views on wealth inequality (this coming from the dude with three houses) were not resonating with those backing the three-testicled, non-binary unicorn running against him.

Yet there was a lesson here that the Biden Administration should (but won't) heed. Lipstick, hormone shots, and high heels shouldn't matter. I can't think of a worse reason to appoint or elect someone to high office than basing the decision on what they look like, where their grandparents were born, or whether they are a man, woman, black, white, or their sexual orientation—*they are of no consequence.* These decisions should rest on a person's character, their values, ethics, qualifications, experience, performance, and abilities. I'll let you decide which is the more intelligent path.

Liars on both sides of the aisle

A hysterical Congressional storm erupted over Representative-elect George Santos (R-NY), who admitted to lying on his résumé while campaigning for Congress. He lied about working at Morgan Stanley and Goldman Sachs, which is kind of stupid since those facts can readily be verified.

Still, he deliberately lied in not one but two separate interviews. Got to admit, he has brass balls thinking he can get away with it. But it's nice to know there are liars on both sides of the aisle—kind of balances things out. Since he was caught red-handed lying to America, I say, "*Can him!*" and let him learn to drive a street sweeper.

We think it's good, but it might kill you

I take issue with all these TV commercials from America's pharmaceutical companies for new drugs with horrendous side effects.

Like new prescription Zablotnik, designed to lower the incidence of stinky toes. Don't use it if you are allergic to its ingredients. Side effects include uncontrolled vomiting, dizziness, memory loss, or death. Why on earth would folks risk death to get rid of stinky feet?

Or what about drugs such as Ucrackhor for the treatment of heart irregularities? The possible side effects include hysterical flatulence, inability to maintain an erection, suicidal thoughts, uncontrolled acne, and blindness.

If you want nightmares, watch prescription drug commercials. My advice? Just say no!

(While I did make up the drugs described above, you get the point!)

630 and 2,600 should scare the pants off of you

No, these are not random numbers I made up. On December 1, 2022, WTTW News[22] reported that Chicago had experienced 630 homicides and 2,600 shootings in 2022—and they still had thirty days until the end of the year! On any given weekend, past Mayor Lightfoot's city racks up *a dozen or two dozen* shootings. Yes, I know Chicago is a cool place with great jazz clubs, outrageous deep-dish pizza, and crooked politicians—but hey, I will never step foot there again because I am deeply allergic to bullets entering my body.

You gotta love Gus

A great BIG shout-out to Congressman Gus Bilirakis for voting for common sense bills that Democrats can't seem to grasp. On what planet would it be okay to draw down our Strategic Petroleum Reserves (SPR)—the reserves held by the United States for emergencies—and sell them to the Chinese? Thank you, Gus, for co-sponsoring and voting for Protecting America's Strategic Petroleum Reserve from China Act.

Renegade idea of the week

I am a fierce proponent of law enforcement, the military, and our heroic veterans. And yes, I do put my money where my mouth is. In addition to supporting organizations such as Wounded Warrior Project, the Gary Sinise Foundation, The USO, and the Tunnel to Towers Foundation, on multiple occasions I have befriended local eateries—through discussions with their owners, I have purchased scores of meals for local law enforcement. It's my way of letting them know they are appreciated. *Consider paying the idea forward in your town.*

NOTABLE AND QUOTABLE

When will American voters stop being stupid?

—Anonymous

Will your retirement strategy survive the Democrats' incessant plans for income and wealth equality?

—Rodger Friedman

MEMO # 16

Are Republicans fiscally demented?

There are no free lunches

I'm flabbergasted—AND I don't say that lightly—that a handful of cities are now eliminating bus fares. In fact, Washington, D.C., has enacted a zero-fare bus bill into law, eliminating the two-dollar bus fare for all.

Folks will be able to ride city buses in D.C. for free. Rich, poor, sleeping on the bus, going to the ballgame, commuting to and from work—all on the taxpayers' dime.

The Council hails it as *transformative* for public transportation. I have a slightly different view. As Adrian Rodgers is purported to have said (and it's not at all clear), the government cannot give to one group of people without taking from another group of people.

So now all taxpayers in Washington, D.C. (a truly dysfunctional armpit of a city where I lived for a number of years) will foot the bill so Joe and Jane Cheapskate can get around for free. Hey, no one else gets around for free. Why should they? The Metro System will still need millions of dollars to run the system, pay the bus drivers, and maintain the buses. AND the folks who ride the Metro will not contribute to footing the bill. *What's wrong with this?*

The D.C. Council fails to understand that **there are no free lunches**. If you are receiving a benefit such as a ride to work or the movies, you are expected to pay for it. It's not free just because a bunch of liberal Democrats waved their magic wand.

The teenage permanent Left

Seems a number of House Democrats are pushing to amend the Constitution to allow sixteen-year-olds to vote. By now you know me well enough to know that I have a problem with this. Why don't we put on a hypothetical debate between these dozen Congressional twits and twelve of our founding fathers? I don't know a single sixteen-year old who wouldn't vote for Taylor Swift or Kim Kardashian. I would not let one drive my daughter to Starbucks, much less give them the right to participate in choosing our nation's leaders. Kelly Clarkson for Senate! Beyoncé for Congress! Kardashian for President! Yeah, that will work out just peachy.

And just so there is no confusion—this is an attempt by the left to abolish the Twenty-Sixth Amendment to the Constitution which allows United States citizens to vote if they are at least eighteen years of age for the express purpose of cementing a left-leaning liberal Democratic majority that will keep them in power indefinitely. A one-party state, sound familiar?

My take? Choose from any of the following:

- Line up these members of Congress and tar and feather them.

- Strip the *knuckleheads* naked, slather honey on them, and drop them off in bear country, preferably high in the Smoky Mountains of Tennessee, duct-taped to a tree.

- Fire them all, send them to Venezuela, and burn their passports (my personal favorite).

One last item, and then we'll move on. Congress was elected by the people as their representatives to solve the nation's problems by legislating solutions to problems such as the collapse of the southern border, rampant crime in our cities, the fentanyl crisis, and protecting our way of life. Best they work on America's most pressing problems rather than on nitwit ideas to solidify their grip on power. Ask any parent who is fearful of their sixteen-year-old driving if that child is mature enough to vote. My guess is that you won't like the answer.

Biden's nastiness on display for all

Going into the debt ceiling fight, President Biden called Republicans fiscally demented. Wow! Now that's a way for President Brandon to come out swinging—call half of Americans fiscally demented. I was speechless at the words coming out of our leader's mouth. His policies have led us to unprecedented economic woes and trillions more in national debt—oh, and forty-year high inflation and all the other idiotic outcomes from an administration that couldn't shoot straight if they tried.

This opening volley to draw attention to the House of Representatives and its uncouth and mean-spirited policies of reining in an out-of-control monetary and fiscal policy is laughable. Yes, Mr. Biden, the House will drag you and your allies on the carpet and beat some fiscal sense into you. If they have to shut down the government, well, it's not the first time, and it won't be the last. And we're all still here.

Another imbecile trying an end run around the First Amendment

Sheila Jackson, a Congresswoman and Democratic imbecile from Texas, has introduced legislation (H.R. 61) titled "Leading against White Supremacy Act of 2023," the so-called LAWS Act. According to Eric Utter, writing for the *American Thinker* on January 17, 2023:[23]

Sheila Jackson Lee (D-TX) has introduced a bill that could make political criticism of non-white individuals by white people a federal crime.

You read that correctly. By the way, would political criticism of a white person by a non-white person remain legal?

The convoluted—yet potentially extremely dangerous—bill proposes that a white person who "vilifies" any non-white person, and whose words subsequently end up on social media, could themselves be guilty of committing a federal crime if those words were accessible by "persons who are predisposed to engaging in any action in furtherance of a white supremacy inspired hate crime." Huh?

If anyone cares to send Ms. Sheila a copy of the Constitution and highlight the First Amendment, I will pay the postage.

Stick to your knitting

I try my best to stay out of the arguments surrounding string theory, neutrinos, and theoretical frameworks involving one-dimensional particles. Why? Because I don't know what I don't know. I stick to my knitting—political satire and retirement investment strategies.

I was told that one of the Dallas Cowboys, Michah Parsons, was discussing, in the media, his thoughts on inflation. Well now, I suppose if Mr. Parsons were to stick to his knitting, he would spend his days doing what football linebackers do rather than holding interviews on inflation and the cost of goods at the supermarkets.

I doubt Dallas hired him for his expertise in monetary policy.

HOV lane shenanigans

I did a double take when I read an article in the January 14, 2023, issue of the *Washington Examiner*. The title of the article was "Virginia Bill Would Consider Fetuses as Car Passengers in HOV (high-occupancy vehicle) lanes."[24] Virginia's House bill 1894 might make for some interesting reading if you have nothing whatsoever to do.

I don't know what's more intriguing—that a fetus is counted as a passenger or that this absurdity is considered noteworthy news.

Take that, Kalifornia!

You may have heard that Kalifornia has passed legislation to outlaw gasoline-powered vehicles by 2035. With the idea that turnabout is fair play, Wyoming state legislators have advanced a bill to phase out electric vehicles (EVs) by 2035. The date of the phase-out deliberately coincides with Kalifornia's law to phase out gasoline-powered vehicles. While we often consider Texas, Louisiana, and North Dakota premier oil- and gas-producing states, Wyoming is an oil and gas titan that employs thousands of people.

Billion $$ loss on electric cars—thousands out of
work as mgt. follows Biden Administration guidance

Renegade idea of the week

The line of succession spells out what happens should the president of the United States die or be impeached while in office. The top spot would go to Kamala Harris—perhaps the most incompetent and disliked vice president in recent history. BUT were Ms. Harris impeached along with Mr. Biden, the top spot would fall to the Speaker of the House. All in all, not a bad outcome. So, don't hope for one impeachment. Hope for two!

NOTABLE AND QUOTABLE

We must reject the idea that every time a law's broken, society is guilty rather than the lawbreaker. It is time to restore the American precept that each individual is accountable for his actions.

—President Ronald Reagan

MEMO # 17

President Biden: I accept your invitation

Noteworthy knuckleheads

How the hell are you supposed to protect your PII (personally identifiable information) when one of the leading cell phone providers falls prey to hackers who make off with personal data files for 37 million customers? Yeah, and don't tell me that an idiot VP of technology left their laptop in the car while shopping at T.J. Maxx and having lunch at IHOP. Perhaps if they spent more money on cyber security and less on glitzy TV commercials, the hackers would have never gotten into their files.

The French are going bananas because Mr. Macron's government is attempting to raise the country's retirement age from sixty-two to sixty-four by 2030. The government says it is the only way to preserve the country's pension system and strengthen the military without resorting to tax increases or additional debt.

France's plan is actually sound. The only problem is that the French hate to work. After all, their retirement age was fifty-eight and then crept up over the years. There are some sound economics going on behind the scenes. Perhaps the French government looked at our $33 trillion in debt and said, "Oh crap! We need to find another way." Of course, the unions have vowed to block Mr. Macron's plan.

I'm not a tweeter—never have been, but I'm told that the Speaker of the House tweeted this to the president, and it was reported in the nation's media:

President Biden: I accept your invitation to sit down and discuss a responsible debt ceiling increase to address irresponsible government spending. I look forward to our meeting.

This is a superbly well-crafted communication that accomplishes several objectives. First, the speaker graciously accepts the president's invitation to sit down and discuss a very important subject. Second, he states that he desires a dialogue regarding a responsible debt ceiling. Third, he hints that such a meeting would not be necessary in the absence of irresponsible government spending.

What's not to like about this guy?

Did you look in the microwave?

Do surprises never end? The media informs us of additional classified documents found in President Biden's home. Seems like Sleepy Joe squirreled away a host of secret documents as mementos of his time as second banana to Oh-Bama. Were I heading up the investigation, I would not stop at the garage or the shoebox under Joe's bed. I'd look in the freezer, the microwave, and behind the hot water heater.

Word has it that state dinner menus were found in a bathroom, a dossier on Kim Jong Un was found in the hall linen closet under a bunch of old (and I mean really old) *Playboy* magazines, and NATO's list of unpaid dues was found in the trunk of Biden's Corvette. Hence the new media buzz phrase—the *Corvette Files.*

Say it ain't true!

Have you heard that a huge number of Americans are sinking into recession oblivion because the fees at their local bank are high? While I find this improbable, folks do have the power of choice. Having spent a significant part of my life in finance (1980 to the present), I still wonder about the average American sacrificing recession preparedness. Exactly what the hell does that mean? It's about as clear as a San Francisco early morning fog.

Preparing for a recession means different things to different people. Generally, you would take the logical path of cutting expenses. For example, Bank A has high fees for their accounts, so you fire them and go to Bank B that has more reasonable fees. Don't let the stock market scare the pants off of you. Create a strategy and have someone to talk to. Also, continue saving, create and stick to a budget, get your finances in order, continue to pay down debt, and remember—it's not the end of the world. It is a normal part of the economic cycle. And just so there is no confusion—I am not giving investment advice!

Don't cry for me, Morgan Stanley

I was told that CEO James Gorman got a 10 percent pay cut in 2022. He now earns a paltry $121,153.84 per day. That's a cool $31.5 million per year for a guy with shiny hair.

Not your grandpa's union

I'm told that joining unions is very popular among federal, state, and local government workers. For those of you who presume I skipped civics class in high school to go across the street for a potato knish and hot dog (sixty-five cents), well I did sometimes. But I stuck around long enough to learn that unions were created to protect and defend workers' interests from their unscrupulous bosses in early industrialized America.

Oddly enough it seems that unions are most popular with government workers. Hmm, what does that say about modern unions protecting their rank-and-file workers from abusive local, state, and federal government bosses?

Renegade idea

It's amazing how we often go through life ignorant of important historical facts. For example, John D. Rockefeller Sr. (1839–1937) and the Standard Oil Trust were the primary reasons for the creation of the trust-busting Sherman Anti-Trust Act of 1890.

Yet most folks are totally unaware of Rockefeller's deep reverence and connection to Black education and Baptist education.

The most **reviled** and **hated** industrialist in U.S. history, Rockefeller was responsible for the lion's share of philanthropy that allowed Spelman College to grow and flourish. The historically Black women's school, named after Rockefeller's wife, Laura Spelman Rockefeller, received Rockefeller's initial $250 contribution in 1883, allowing it to move out of a dank church basement to a sprawling nine-acre campus. Over the years, Rockefeller and his foundation contributed more than $25 million to the school to improve and support African American education.

Oh, and by the way, today's University of Chicago was born with Standard Oil profits and would not be in existence without Mr. Rockefeller's sizable philanthropy.

NOTABLE AND QUOTABLE

**If you're a GIVER, remember to learn your limits—
because the TAKERS don't have any!**

—Henry Ford

**We need leaders who are basically thinking about
the shareholders and their employees, and how well
the shareholders are doing and their employees.
And I think today it's all about woke diversity,
things that don't hit the bottom line.**

—Bernie Marcus, co-founder, The Home Depot

I trust dividends paid on time and in cash.

—Rodger A. Friedman, retirement strategist and political satirist

MEMO # 18

We know who you are, and we're coming for your money

Extraterrestrial gas

News of a radio signal detected from nine billion light years away from Earth captured the public's imagination recently. NASA was all beside itself trying to figure out everything about the signal. As near as they can tell, the signal spelled out an order for two Whoppers with extra sauce and no onions, a chocolate shake, and large fries. Evidently, onions give the extraterrestrials gas.

We know who you are, and we're coming for your money

The Kalifornia Assembly needs a finance course—not more taxing authority.

AB-259 is not a new mouthwash, a deodorant for *down there*, or a new iPhone. It's Kalifornia's Assembly Bill 259 that allows the state . . . are you ready . . . to provide for the taxation of all forms of personal property or wealth.

The new wealth tax was introduced into the Kalifornia Assembly on January 19, 2023, by a gaggle of left-wing Democrats intent on feeding the beast of state government spending. The law would go after income as well as assets, realized, and unrealized appreciation. The resolution seeks an amendment to the state's Constitution.

Interestingly, the resolution begins with six *whereas* paragraphs. I assume they read something like this:

- Whereas, we need more money, and we know you got it.

- Whereas, some folks (those who work hard) have more money than others.

- Whereas, we intend to soak the rich and give to everyone who is not rich.

- Whereas, we want the rich to pay their fair share.

- Whereas, we have guns and the power to take your money.

- Whereas, you are powerless to stop us.

- Whereas, we know who you are and where you live.

What the Kalifornia legislators fail to recognize is simple economics. *Hey, control your spending.* I'm certain these folks would be surprised that should this ridiculous resolution actually become law, a host of wealthy folks will hightail it for Texas, Tennessee, and Florida, leaving the left-wing legislators groveling in the dust. I have no love for this state and shall never step foot in it.

A debt crisis makes for sneaky tax authorities

Back in 2010 during the Greek debt crisis, the *Los Angeles Times* ran an interesting article about swimming pools—specifically swimming pools in Greece and more specifically swimming pools in Greece that were not taxed.[25] You see, in Greece, home swimming pools were considered a luxury, one that influences tax status. While 300-odd pool owners ponied up the required tax, a hefty 17,000 or so did not. It seems that tax avoidance is both an art form, a sport, and a national pastime in Greece.

So, with the help of government helicopter overflights of wealthy neighborhoods, as well as Google Earth photos, Greek tax authorities were able to find the scofflaws and tax the hell out of them. So, the next time you are taking a soak in the pool, look up and smile because odds are, you're being photographed!

Is this a Florida thing, or is it everywhere?

While commuting to the office, I spy signs that say, "CBD Kratom." Mind you, I believe that CBD has something to do with pot. Kratom? No clue. Sounds like one of those made-up words (aren't all words made up?) like Kleenex or Xerox that found its way into our lexicon big-time. Stores that sell this stuff are all over the place like tattoo parlors (don't get me started). My guess is that all the customers are under thirty, into the CBD culture, and happy to fork over their money.

Let's shrug—shall we?

Today's political environment was foretold with great accuracy in the 1950s.

How **Ayn Rand** was able to nail today's dysfunctional autocratic dystopia with such great accuracy is nothing short of astounding. Her 1957 grand novel, *Atlas Shrugged*, laid out in great detail a government intent on curtailing economic freedoms right out of Elizabeth Warren's playbook. Rand was a fervent proponent of capitalism, property rights, and the individual's freedom to live their life without government interference. The book takes a deep dive into burdensome regulations designed to stifle competition and transfer increasing amounts of capital from the private sector to the Federal Treasury.

I recommend the book without reservation, and when you're done, throw it at the head of the nearest social Democrat (just kidding). The 1,200-page tome might knock some sense into them. That's doubtful, but hey, it's worth a try.

Congressman Archie Bunker

Many of us remember the television comedy *All in the Family*. You might recall Carroll O'Connor's brilliant portrayal of Archie Bunker, the World War II vet and blue-collar factory worker. He was a small-minded bigot who lived in Queens, New York, and always had something nasty to say about someone or groups of someones. No one was spared his irrational anger toward Jews, African Americans, hippies, the Nixon White House, and practically all America west of the Hudson River.

Bunker was known to speak irrationally on many subjects, but politics got him hot under the collar more often than anything else. It seems the House of Representatives has its own version of Archie Bunker—a Democrat by the name of Hakeem Jeffries. Shortly after the media circus when Kevin McCarthy finally scored enough votes to be named Speaker of the House, Jeffries was quoted as saying, "I'll be blunt—Republicans are incapable of governing."

Well, Mr. Hakeem *Archie Bunker* Jeffries, congratulations! You now have a significant number of Americans who believe you are a *jackass*, incapable of prudent and rational thought. To mouth off in such an unprofessional manner is an affront and an insult to the United States, and you owe the American people an apology.

Hooray for Captain Obvious

During an interview in January 2023 with Maria Bartiromo,[26] Senator Manchin (D-WV) characterized the debt ceiling impasse in the following terms: "I think what we have to do is realize that we have a problem. We have a debt problem." Ya think, Senator? Is that what you're paid the big bucks for, to state the obvious? The federal deficit smacks of a sixteen-year-old drunken tenth grader maxing out his dad's Master Card buying expensive stuff for all his friends and later wrapping his father's prize Corvette around a telephone pole.

Will someone pull this idiot away from the microphone?

While White House Press Secretary Karine Jean-Pierre was defending the White House's hard stance about the federal debt ceiling, she evidently and very un-ladylike grew a big pair of brass balls and proclaimed, "There will not be any negotiations over the debt ceiling."

Well, then, I guess this unelected lady has the final word. Let's stay tuned, shall we?

Break the law—get to vote

Connecticut legislators are pushing for a new law allowing illegal aliens the right to vote in state elections. Gee, I thought the right to vote was reserved for citizens. Guess my degree in political science isn't worth the parchment it's printed on.

Renegade idea

Popular morons have now identified sixty-eight different genders. Not to be rude—**well, of course I mean to be rude**—but I put forth that there are only two genders. They're the ones we all learned about in grade school, the ones printed on our birth certificates, vaccine records, voting cards, driver's licenses, and passports.

When did an illegal alien become an *undocumented immigrant*? After all, we are talking about an individual whose first act upon setting foot in the United States was to commit a felony.

NOTABLE AND QUOTABLE

It will be of little avail to the people, that the laws
are made by men of their own choice, if the laws be
so voluminous that they cannot be read, or so
incoherent that they cannot be understood; if they
be repealed or revised before they are promulgated,
or undergo such incessant changes that no man,
who knows what the law is today, can guess what it
will be tomorrow. Law is defined to be a rule of action;
but how can that be a rule, which is little known,
and less fixed?

— James Madison, Founding Father, President of the United States

MEMO # 19

A biblical opportunity for the
Squad to provide sanctuary

I like how this guy thinks

Word has it that Congressman Pat Fallon of Texas has a thought-provoking idea to pass on to Texas Governor Greg Abbott on how to grab the attention of Democrats intent on flooding our country with illegal aliens.

The Congressman has mentioned numerous times that the overwhelming majority seeking entry into the Unites States are economic migrants, not asylum-seekers.

Fallon has suggested that illegals be voluntarily bussed to Senator Chuck Schumer's home in New York and to Nancy Pelosi's fortress estate in San Francisco. Might I add that members of *the Squad* might also be included as a destination, although as new Congresspersons, they might invite the visitors to sack out on sofas in their tiny apartments and share a bathroom with them.

In my mind, Squad members—especially Representatives Ilhan Omar of Minnesota, Alexandria Ocasio-Cortez of New York, Rashida Tlaib of Michigan, and Ayanna Pressley of Massachusetts—will have the biblical opportunity to provide food, blankets, and sanctuary up close and personal. That ought to remove the grins of their faces rather fast.

This is definitely NOT a socialist paradise!

What was a pity is now a national disgrace

When did America become so divisive? If you have trouble wrapping your brain around this concept, try substituting the words *discordant*, *conflict-ridden*, *contentious*, or *acrimonious*. Daily papers (and online media) are filled with one group *ripping* or *bashing* another, one politician (including those in the White House) *tearing apart* those with opposing viewpoints. Any pretense of civility has long ago vanished. What's a pity is that we used to read this on page twenty-seven of the daily paper, now it's the headline on page one—and a national disgrace.

Russia, China, Iran, North Korea, and others must be giving each other *high-fives* as they watch us expend our energies and national assets fighting each other rather than challenging their misdeeds. When did we become a nation fraught with such animosity toward each other? I suspect it was when liberal Democrats stole the show that things began to shift toward untold levels of brinkmanship (Uh oh! Call the word police—the word *man* is in the word *brinkmanship* and should be replaced with a gender-neutered word).

It is now commonplace to hear the president, senators, and House members call portions of the country who disagree with them idiots, stupid, fascist, racist, and more. This is not the America I know. Their outright condescension has reached a fever pitch as they appear to never tire of lecturing Conservatives and Republicans alike how antiquated their attitudes are and how a new system of laws needs to be instituted. This is not hollow rhetoric, this is today's cancel culture on steroids, devoid of tolerance for ideas other than their own. You can't make this stuff up. *I call on all who read these words to help vote out of office the ignorant politicians who have infected our government and replace them with thoughtful, intelligent, ethical, and prudent decision-makers to act as stewards of our future freedom and liberty.*

Now that's a GREAT quote!

Billionaire investor Ray Dalio, founder of Bridgewater Associates, called the debt limit ceiling a farce. He was quoted as saying, "It's a farce that works like a bunch of alcoholics who write laws to enforce drinking limits."

Prying loose entrenched politicians

On January 23, 2023, Senator Ted Cruz (R-TX) introduced a Constitutional amendment to impose term limits for Congress.[27] The amendment would limit U.S. senators to two six-year terms and members of the U.S. House of Representatives to three two-year terms.

Senator Cruz said:

Term limits are critical to fixing what's wrong with Washington, D.C. The Founding Fathers envisioned a government of citizen legislators who would serve for a few years and return home, not a government run by a small group of special interests and lifelong, permanently entrenched politicians who prey upon the brokenness of Washington to govern in a manner that is totally unaccountable to the American people.

Here are a couple cases in point:

- Nancy Pelosi has represented San Francisco, California's 12th District in Congress for nearly thirty-three years. At age eighty-three, she is again running for Congress in 2024. The founders, if alive today, would tell her, "Nancy, go home!"

- Steny Hoyer (D-MD) has served forty years in the House of Representatives. Hey, Congressman, time to hang up your Congressional tie and go home.

- Senator Chuck Schumer (D-NY) has served for forty-one years. Don't let the door hit your ass on the way out, Chuck. Your grandchildren miss you, and we won't.

- Senator Diane Feinstein (D-CA) recently passed away after holding her Senate seat for thirty years. Truth be told, she should have entered a nursing home long before she passed as she was unable to fulfill the duties of her office in a manner befitted a U.S. Senator

Bravo, Congresspersons! Now comes the hard part. What do you think the chances are of this amendment to the U.S. Constitution actually becoming the law of the land? Well, *maybe we Americans can give it a push by letting our elected officials know that if they don't vote for the amendment, we—the American people—will vote them out of office.* That ought to get their attention.

It's been said that Americans get what they deserve. I believe that. And they also get what they vote for. Americans just keep electing *jackasses* like those mentioned above.

Why do we care?

The media is in love with the idea of reporting useless crap. For example, on one of the many occasions that Tesla stock went into the toilet, the talking heads were shouting how many billions Elon Musk lost on that particular day. Sometime later, when Tesla announced good news, these same talking heads were smiling and high-fiving each other how many billions Musk had made in just a couple of days. So what?

Not only do the media have an incredibly short memory but they also stick to the mistaken belief that random facts carry any weight. So why would I care how much the Earth weighs or how many molecules are in a scoop of gelato? When will the media finally get it in their heads that we just don't care and that they should pursue real news?

Random thoughts

In keeping with our mythically functioning government, perhaps America should adopt the unicorn, a mythical beast, as our mascot. Perhaps the American flag could be redesigned with a rainbow-colored unicorn in the center of the ol' stars and stripes. That way we could show the world that we are inclusive, diverse, equitable, and sensitive to LBTGQ, etc.

If you are a frequent flyer, you may have noticed that flight attendants at many airlines can now choose uniforms of whatever gender they prefer. So, don't be surprised if Nicholas, the bearded flight attendant, is wearing a dress and stockings. Makes me wonder if it is permissible for female crewmembers to wear their jock straps on the outside . . .

Renegade idea

The government didn't listen to me when I suggested during the height of the pandemic and ultra-low interest rates that they—the U.S. Treasury—should issue fifty-year and one hundred-year treasury bonds, locking in borrowing costs for decades at ridiculously low interest rates. Instead, they kept to their knitting, issuing T-Bills that mature in less than 365 days and five-year T-Notes. God forbid that the government would do something intelligent to lower the massive borrowing costs incurred by persistent and excessive government spending. And no, I am not giving investment advice to the United States Treasury, although it appears that someone should.

NOTABLE AND QUOTABLE

Posterity—you will never know how much it has cost my generation to preserve your freedom. I hope you will make good use of it.

—John Quincy Adams sixth President of the United States

If we are to have another contest in the near future of our national existence, I predict that the dividing line will not be Mason and Dixon's but between patriotism and intelligence on the one side, and superstition, ambition, and ignorance on the other.

—Ulysses S. Grant eighteenth President of the United States, Commanding General of the Union Army

MEMO # 20

A recipe to destroy the United States

Have you noticed?

I have noticed an alarming trend over the years as financial pundits on the popular daytime stock market TV shows have adopted the sports model of *play-by-play* action. My guess is that their strategy is to get you hooked on watching minute-by-minute changes in the NASDQ, the DOW, and the S&P. Unless you are a professional trader (I am not) you don't care if the market is up twelve points or twenty-one points. I guess they would love to get everyone hooked on this like a crack cocaine addict so they can charge more for advertising.

And, have you noticed the little countdown timers in the corner of the screen? They count down how many minutes till a Fed announcement, a Bureau of Labor Statistics news release or some other arcane piece of news. Yes, these announcements can and do move the market, but I suggest that a better use of your time is to hug your kids, pay your mortgage, or kiss your spouse.

What a load of crap

Watching the TV news can be hazardous to your health. I don't do it often, but on one occasion I heard that the debt standoff in Congress was an attack on democracy. House Republicans were calling for fiscal restraint. How that is considered an attack on democracy is beyond my pay grade.

I guess that liberal cretins don't believe in *living within one's means* and being financially responsible with taxpayers' money. So much for an assault...

Who knew we had so much in common?

I have long admired Warren Buffet's investment skill and philosophy even though Harvard Business School turned him down as a potential student. But until recently, I had no idea that we have so much in common, including the following:

- We both earned the prestigious Mechanical Pencil Award from the Dale Carnegie Institute for public speaking.

- Warren and I both went to college in New York.

- We both took girls on dates to the Uptown Theater in Washington, D.C.

How to destroy the United States

- Support massive unchecked illegal immigration
- Allow illegals to vote in elections
- Open our borders
- Place state elections under Federal Government control
- Defund the police and the military
- Encourage discrimination
- Flood the country with money by printing trillions of dollars
- Spend, spend, spend—run up the national debt

- Surrender our energy independence
- Encourage infighting between states
- Violate the United States Constitution
- Pack the Supreme Court

I ask you, how many of these are the Biden Administration and Congressional Democrats trying to achieve?

Want an out-of-this-world spot?

It seems that NASA's James Webb Space Telescope has found a nice out-of-this-world spot that Zillow would love to sell you. The LHS 475 b is an Earth-sized exoplanet located just a hop, skip, and a jump from Earth approximately forty-one light years away. Before you call your real estate broker for a prime spot, you might want to wait until NASA verifies the existence of an atmosphere. Then you'll be good to go!

Swift fiasco

Apparently, the United States Senate and many of their staff members are deeply concerned about getting tickets to Taylor Swift concerts. They have called for hearings, questioning Live Nation Entertainment (the merger of Ticketmaster and Live Nation). Word has it that staffers were hoping for an impromptu concert in the hearing room by a scantily clad Taylor Swift, complete with selfies at day's end.

NOTABLE AND QUOTABLE

"Do not underestimate the unimportance of practically everything.

— John Maxwell, American author and leadership speaker

Attention and focus are the IQ of the 21st century.

—Lee Milteer, best-selling author, entrepreneur, visionary, and my friend

MEMO # 21

New England freezes without Trinidad

If you think things have gone too far, you're right

Case in point: The London School of Economics traces its roots to 1895. Much has changed in over one hundred years, yet my guess is that microeconomics, macroeconomics, inflation, monetary and fiscal policy are still taught there. Some things just don't change. But, in 2023, the famed school decided to do away with Christmas and Easter holiday breaks and not recognize them on their official schedule. Seems the woke of the world have taken over. I wouldn't be surprised to see sixty-eight separate bathrooms for all supposed sixty-eight genders . . .

Case in point: Some folks are just plain crackers. We all love and remember Scooby-Doo, the kids cartoon show. Seems HBO cannot leave well enough alone. It's created a redo of the character Velma in her own show—a lesbian, pole-dancing detective—and it has the media up in arms. Believe it or not, some are arguing that Velma's character doesn't provide the depth of lesbian sexuality needed for a convincing performance. What is more ridiculous? The news reporting this or me writing about it? 'Nuff said . . .

Case in point: Walmart raised its minimum wage to fourteen dollars per hour, a 17 percent increase over its previous wage scale.

I don't know where you come from, but a 17 percent increase ain't just fluff. It's real money. That comes on the heels of Delta Airlines giving its pilots a 34 percent raise and railroad engineers getting a 25 percent increase. These are huge raises in my book. Yet Bernie Sanders, the senator from the Banana Republic of Vermont, droned on and on how it is not enough. Hey, Bernie! Ever hear of wage push inflation? Go back and crack an economics book.

Have you noticed that this acronym keeps growing? (LGBTQIA2S+)

Eric Utter penned an unusually fascinating piece in *American Thinker* on February 1, 2023.[28] The article, "University Offers 'Unconditional Love Fund' . . . as Long as You're Not Heterosexual," portrays how utterly nuts selected select institutions of higher education have become. Should you doubt this, here is a quote from Mr. Utter's article:

> *Michigan State University (MSU) is now offering an "Unconditional Love Fund" to its young scholars . . . on one condition: a student must be a member of the LGBT community in order to apply for the money. The fund's purported purpose is to 'provide LGBTQIA2S+ Michigan State University students with flexible assistance in a timely manner to address extraordinary and unexpected financial hardships associated with their sexual and/or gender identity. Selected students will be given up to $500.*

Seattle City Council learns that feeling safe TRUMPS everything

Seems a majority of Seattle's City Council is considering quitting after residents are up in arms over their nutcase liberal policies.

Well, you don't have to be a rocket scientist to learn that seven of nine council members will not seek reelection. It seems residents are upset and threatening council members over the huge increases in crime and homelessness. Clearly, backing a "defund the police philosophy" has proved NOT to be in the best interests of Seattle's citizens.

Perhaps Seattle's crime crisis will end with the election of prudent citizens who value the safety of the community over militant actions such as defunding the police. Maybe they will bring an end to the destruction of businesses and loss of faith in a once beautiful city that is now a national disgrace.

Just what we need—a larger Congress

A bill introduced by Democrat Congressman Earl Blumenauer of Oregon would add 150 additional seats to the House of Representatives, increasing its size from the current 435 established in 1929 to 585. Inasmuch as Congress is one of the more hated institutions in our country, I'm not a proponent of adding another 150 Congresspeople to screw things up more than they already have.

New England freezes without Trinidad

Political simpletons at the state and federal levels deserve a second write-up due to their ongoing stupidity, bickering, and poor planning. As readers of *The Sunday Memo* know, New England pays exorbitant prices for natural gas due to a lack of pipelines connecting their region to massive supplies available cheaply in the rest of the country.

New England political loons (pardon me, esteemed legislators) continue to block the construction of needed natural gas pipelines to their region. There is only one solution—suspend or do away with the Jones Act that limits state-to-state transport of anything if the ship is not built, owned, operated, and flying the U.S. flag. Worse yet, fewer than one hundred ships across the country qualify under the law.

The Jones Act was created in 1920, over one hundred years ago when the world was very different than it is today. This archaic relic of a bygone era needs to go the way of kerosene lamps. Until then, Trinidad provides the cheapest alternative to New England during freezing winters.

By the way, Trinidad is the largest oil and gas producer in the Caribbean. Hey, blockheads, ever hear of the **Marcellus shale formation**? It's located in New York, Ohio, Pennsylvania, Maryland, New Jersey, and Virginia. The U.S. Geological Survey estimates that there are 214 trillion cubic feet of natural gas contained in the formation.

According to the U.S. Energy Information Administration there is enough natural gas in the formation to provide for over one hundred years of our energy needs.

Yet two terminals in Massachusetts rely on LNG (liquid natural gas) shipped from Trinidad, 2,200 miles away, so people don't freeze to death in the winter. Has everyone lost their minds?

Disingenuous is an appropriate term to describe White House behavior

The Merriam-Webster Dictionary defines *disingenuous* as "lacking in candor, giving a false appearance of simple frankness; calculating." More to the point, it might contain elements of truth but is delivered with the intent to deceive.

It's very interesting to watch an institution such as the White House speak out of two sides of its mouth simultaneously. Our fearless Mr. Biden speaks about weaning our country off its fossil oil dependence while chiding the oil industry for not investing in producing more oil. In reality, the major oil companies are raising shareholder dividends, buying back stock, and drilling for oil and gas all at the same time!

Any casual observer of the oil industry will tell you that new projects are often very expensive, costing hundreds of millions or billions of dollars and taking years to come to fruition. Also they must carefully weave their way through numerous challenges such as federal and state regulations, the Army Corps of Engineers, tribal authorities, protests, and lawsuits.

You need look no further than Mr. Obama scuttling the Keystone XL pipeline, Mr. Trump rejuvenating the project, and then Mr. Biden killing it again, all through presidential executive orders. Billions of dollars and ten years were spent on a project that yielded a negative return and never delivered one barrel of oil.

Random thought of the day

If you get a knock on the door and a gentleperson (see, I'm growing) says, "I'm from the government and I'm here to help you," just smile, ask them to wait a brief moment, close the door, and run like hell out the back door. Or as President Ronald Reagan stated so eloquently: *The most terrifying words in the English language are: "I'm from the government and I'm here to help."*

Don't do what this woman did

Reports out of Chicago—a woman has been charged after the body of her ninety-six-year-old mother was found in her freezer. OK . . . this leaves me speechless too.

NOTABLE AND QUOTABLE

Those who enjoy responsibility usually get it; those who merely like exercising authority usually lose it.

—Malcolm Forbes, American publisher,
hot air balloon enthusiast, and billionaire

There is no justification for taking away individuals' freedom in the guise of public safety.

—Thomas Jefferson, U.S. President, draftsman
of the Declaration of Independence

MEMO # 22

A story factory obsessed with eyeball count

Time to grow the hell up

Imagine if you will a twenty-something millennial living at home, earning close to six figures, and having no cash to spare to fund a retirement account. Seems far-fetched? Maybe they have an unending fascination with comic books, childhood trading cards, or other things that captivate them, and those things drain their checking account for unreasonable sums.

It's time a family member sat them down and taught them some financial basics. It's a pity they weren't taught those valuable lessons earlier in life. And in case you're wondering, I blame the kid's parents, their high school, and their college. They all failed in their basic job to groom a person who makes prudent decisions and can stand on their own two feet.

Glad I don't live in Washington, D.C. anymore

Mainstream media reported that the House GOP is planning to vote on overturning a D.C. law allowing illegal aliens to vote in local D.C. elections. It will be interesting to see how this plays out. My take? Only United States citizens should be empowered to vote. You don't violate our laws and then be given voting privileges, welfare money, driver's licenses, and free healthcare. Those privileges, if appropriate, are reserved for law-abiding citizens.

Politicians refuse to recognize that if our country keeps giving away *free stuff* to folks who illegally cross our borders, there will be two billion or so economically disadvantaged people lining up at our shores to take advantage. At that point, we will have equality. In other words, we will all be equally poor and all in bread lines.

Remember, the *free stuff* has to be paid for by someone—and that someone is the American taxpayer.

What's Hallmark going to do now?

Valentine's Day used to be so simple. Man loves woman, woman loves man, find the right card to reflect the right sentiment—sappy, funny, racy, poetic. Pretty simple choices until today. I suppose we now have LBTGQ+ variants as far as the eye can see.

The writers at Hallmark must have their hands full. Okay, John, you write the gay cards. Barbara, you write the non-binary stuff. Jackie, you write the funny lesbian cards. And Jean, you're in charge of all the pan-sexual, flute-playing, polyandrous beings that don't fit into any other category. What a mess!

Tell me it ain't so!

The February 5, 2023, issue of the *Washington Examiner*[29] carried an editorial too frightening to read. For sanity reasons, I will not reveal the author. Just say that she, it, they, them, he, him, whoever postulated, suggested, advanced the notion that Michelle Obama might be the 2024 Democratic nominee for president. Should this come to pass, you may attempt to find me in Panama or Costa Rica 'cause I'm hightailing it the hell out of here.

I spent a fair amount of time deciding what to write about the Chinese weather balloon incident. A U.S. jet shot it out of the sky once it cleared the mainland and was over the Atlantic Ocean. For a while, I thought I would see a report that Hunter Biden shot down the balloon with one of his dad's rifles.

The media had their collective hair on fire with numerous stories, much conjecture, and little fact. But that's what media has become—*a story factory obsessed with eyeball count*—so they can inflate their ad rates and increase their revenues.

Yes, I still love Congressman Gus

I received an update from Congressman, Gus Bilirakis. Here is part of his message:

With $31.4 TRILLION in national debt, we are committed to finding a solution that is reasonable, sensible, and responsible regarding raising the debt ceiling. We must finally address Washington's reckless government spending if we want to put America on a better fiscal path. There is a bipartisan path forward: Instead of refusing to negotiate, Democrats need to join Republicans in crafting a plan that protects taxpayers. President Biden and Senate Democrats would be irresponsible not to negotiate with House Republicans on this important fiscal issue

My comments: Remember when our esteemed leader said he would not negotiate with Republicans on the *"debt crisis"*? Does that mean he doesn't want to work with Republicans in crafting a plan that protects taxpayers? Does that mean he is not committed to finding a solution that is reasonable, sensible, and responsible regarding raising the debt ceiling? See? Spinning words is oh so easy!

NOTABLE AND QUOTABLE

The society that puts equality before freedom will end up with neither. The society that puts freedom before equality will end up with a great measure of both.

—Milton Friedman, Economist and Nobel Prize winner

No one's rights can be secured by the violation of the rights of others.

—Ayn Rand

MEMO # 23

Media insanity: Dominatrix convicted in cheesecake poisoning

Random thoughts

Fox Business reported that the governor of Pennsylvania removed college degree requirements for most state jobs. That seems to be the most intelligent news story I've read in a while. After all, if I'm looking for a job in the cafeteria of the state building, in the mailroom, or fixing copy machines, why the hell do I have to sit through Psych 101 or freshman English? Bravo, Pennsylvania!

A consequence of America's *migrant free-for-all* is news that an Arizona hospital is on the brink of collapse after spending $20 million on migrant care. Yuma Regional Medical Center is in the crosshairs of the crisis since it is in a border town overrun with illegal aliens lacking healthcare. And in case you were wondering, yes, I blame it on Biden not securing our borders.

It was only a matter of time. Some amateur blockhead journalist has coined the term *Balloon Gate.* Should you come across said article, kindly email the author to get a life and stop being so derivative.

Titan: The Life of John D. Rockefeller, Sr. is a fascinating read at 800-plus pages. Maybe listening is more your style—either way, it is

LONG and captivating. Here are a couple of items I picked up about the man and the family that I was clueless about:

- John D. Rockefeller Sr. provided the majority of capital to found the University of Chicago, the Riverside Church in Morningside Heights (NYC), and the Cloisters Museum (NYC).

- John D. Rockefeller Jr. provided the majority of capital to re-create Colonial Williamsburg, Virginia, and the Metropolitan Museum of Art in New York City.

- John D. Rockefeller Jr. was charged with **giving away** the colossal fortune his father created through the creation of the Standard Oil Trust in an amount that was thought to be in excess of $500 million.

So much for billionaires not doing anything for society.

Career update

I'm no Plato, but I was considering switching careers and becoming a philosopher. Don't laugh! My guess is that there is a *philosopher deficit* in the United States, and perhaps more are needed. As I rolled the idea around in my brain, I came up with more questions than answers. For example, would I be able to work from home? Can I wear yoga pants? What about healthcare coverage, a 401(k) plan, and dental insurance? Is there room for advancement? What about franchising opportunities? Should I incorporate to limit liability or go the sole proprietor route like Aristotle? I think I need to table the idea and let it percolate for a while. If you have any ideas, don't be shy, let me know.

Media insanity at the federal level

SCOTUS, POTUS, and now SOTU. I've had it! The media—yes, I'm harping on the media again—can't spell real words and have to make up new ones.

- SCOTUS—Supreme Court of the United States
- POTUS—President of the United States
- COTUS—Congress of the United States
- And last but not least, SOTU—(State of the Union address)

If you have a favorite acronym, keep it to yourself.

More media insanity

Sometimes you see a headline and just have to stop and reread it to make sure you read it correctly the first time. So, compliments to the February 9, 2023, *New York Post.* Here is, word for word, one of the strangest and most absurd headlines I have ever read: "NYC Dominatrix Viktoria Nasyrova Convicted in Cheesecake Poisoning Case."[30]

After reading the article (twice) I felt I had to share my thoughts. Obviously, a few things stand out. First, it's a headline about a dominatrix. You don't see that every day. Next, she was convicted of poisoning someone. We read about poisoning every now and then, especially with international spy services involved—nothing special other than someone was poisoned, and that's a terrible thing. But next, wow! It involved cheesecake! And what did I do? I started thinking about the menu at the Cheesecake Factory. Sometimes my brain just scares me . . .

It seems that Mike Pence is the newest member of the *classified documents Who Me? Club.* Were I the FBI, I would be checking out Kim Kardashian, Whoopi Goldberg, and Moe, Larry, and Curly. They all seem suspicious.

Who knew that New York City politicians blame each other just like Congressional Democrats blame everything on Republicans (and vice versa). Seems Mayor Eric Adams blames prior Mayor Bill de Blasio for illegal alien budget woes. Ain't it grand? The new mayor blames the old mayor for the New York City illegals' migrant crisis and takes no responsibility for his part in it.

Aw, for the love of Pete!

"Aw, for the love of Pete!" My dad used to say that when he was pissed off. I never understood where the saying came from. Anyway, I thought of it when I learned that the Department of Labor may have misspent over $190 billion on Covid unemployment benefits.

For Pete's sake! One hundred ninety billion dollars *might have been misspent?* Not a whole lot of confidence here. We all know that the federal government can't hand out a dollar without fifty cents going to unscrupulous, bad actors. But $190 billion? Do you have any idea how enormous a sum of taxpayer money that is?

This is disgraceful. Of course, many will point to Biden, but I sincerely doubt he was the guy on the corner slipping fifties and C-notes to drug pushers and state enemies. Obviously, a program was put together with haste and without appropriate safeguards to ensure that the funds were disbursed to the intended recipients who were in need. Was it negligence, incompetence, or mindless bureaucratic policies? We may never know, but it's part of the reason I am pissed off every time I send a check to the IRS. That's because *I am more careful with my money than they are with my money.*

Legend? I don't think so

Evidently, General Motors is hyping up its new electric cars with Hollywood actors behind the wheel. Nothing new there, but the media headlines are stretching it a bit when they describe Will Farrell as a *Hollywood legend.* Granted, the guy's funny, but he ain't no Marlon Brando, Humphrey Bogart, Cary Grant, or James Cagney. Sorry, Will.

NOTABLE AND QUOTABLE

The illegal we do immediately.
The unconstitutional takes a little longer.

—Henry A. Kissinger

My country owes me nothing. It gave me, as it gives every boy and girl, a chance. It gave me schooling, independence of action, opportunity for service and honor.

—Herbert Hoover

MEMO # 24

Gender stupidity in New Hampshire

The idiotic interweb

You'll notice that I am again including a section about "Pete." This one is called "Aw, for Pete's sake!" Readers of *The Sunday Memo* might recall that this was one of my dad's favorite expressions. After all these years, I still didn't know what the hell it meant, so I Googled it. Turns out that *Pete* is just a nice substitution for Christ, and the phrase signifies annoyance or frustration. So far, so good. But it made me think of how technology has added to society's stupidity. Now, watch the idiotic *interweb* at work . . .

When you Google "for Pete's sake," you will also see the following entries:

- Shop for Pete's sake on Amazon's official site
- Find for Pete's sake on eBay
- Shop for Pete's sake deals on . . .
- Enjoy discounts and hot sales on for Pete's sake
- For Pete's sake, a unique neighborhood pub (I like that one!)

I guess this is the artificial part of artificial intelligence . . . welcome to the idiotic interweb. Perhaps AI should be short for *artificial idiot?*

Eric Utter wrote a scathing article in *American Thinker* on February 10, 2023, that warranted inclusion in this book. Here's what he wrote:

According to WBFF-TV (Fox 45), the Maryland State Department of Education recently released Baltimore students' 2022 test results, which revealed that an incredible 93 percent of third- through eighth-graders tested below their grade level in math. In fact, after analyzing the results, the Baltimore news station found twenty-three city schools where not a single student tested proficient in math.[31]

Mr. Utter then shared this most probable response by education officials and the Baltimore City Council:

Well, I, for one, smell racism! We must ban mathematics in all its intolerant, non-inclusive, racist, misogynistic, homophobic, and transphobic forms! It is nothing but a dangerous relic of white supremacy!

Bravo, Eric Utter, for raising our awareness that after pouring hundreds of millions of dollars into Baltimore's education system, taxpayers can see that their tax money went right down the sewer. As a former citizen of the Chesapeake state, I want a tax refund, or better test scores from these kids. At a minimum, they should fire all the teachers and administrators, and hire a top-notch educational company to come in and run the schools. After all, they could not do worse than the current crop of incompetents.

By the way, the rest of Maryland doesn't come up smelling like roses either. The Democratic Party controls the governor, secretary of state, attorney general, and both chambers of the Legislature. I am eternally grateful to live in a red state and bid good riddance to the blue Frankenstein known as Maryland.

What we can learn from Kentucky

The Kentucky Senate has passed a bill banning TikTok from state devices. I applaud them and hope every state in the Union follows their lead. As a society, we do not need a popular social media platform bound at the waist with the Chinese Communist Party (CCP). An even better solution is to permanently outlaw the use of TikTok in the United States by everyone, making it unavailable on any and every device. I'm sure millennials can find other platforms to watch cute baby and kitten videos.

New Hampshire lunatics

There is a gender *stupidity* going on in New Hampshire. Fox News reported on February 12, 2023,[32] that students staged a walkout after the school district banned the use of urinals in what were formerly the boys' bathrooms. Good going, kids! I guess everyone now has to sit when they pee because that is . . . equitable?

It's also ridiculous, outrageous, stupid, and harebrained. I fully expect the intellectually challenged politicians in the New Hampshire Legislature to pass a resolution declaring that all people, regardless of their sixty-eight genders, should have identical bodily plumbing and that it is a horrendous miscarriage of justice that all biological genitalia are not equal.

Why can't New Hampshire be more like Wyoming with a majority of Republicans, all permitted to carry firearms and have delightful, soul-searching conversations with the Democratic minority as they point the way to those big green highway signs that lead to other states?

I don't trust Chuck Schumer not to spit in my latte

Schumer is up to his usual inane accusations. Remember Kevin McCarthy's attempts to clean up the operations of the U.S. House of Representatives and his discussions with Mr. Biden that we must enter into debt ceiling negotiations in hopes of reaching a responsible and fiscally prudent compromise? Recall that Sir Biden scolded the House leader that there would be no negotiations on the debt ceiling.

After reading the *Washington Examiner* article posted on February 12, 2023,[33] asserting that Schumer was quoted as saying, "Is it Social Security and Medicare? That would hurt the American people." I felt I needed to tell you my takeaway. Schumer's pronouncement came after House leadership said that cuts to Medicare and Social Security are off the table. Senator Schumer is famous for putting words in people's mouths and acting deceitully. Were he a barista at Starbucks, I would double-count my change after making sure he didn't spit in my latté. And here's my tip for Mr. Schumer: Stop lying to the American public.

Give it a rest

There is no shortage of groups, activists, and city councils to beat the drum and protest against a name, a team, or an object. The latest assault is against Super Bowl Champs the Kansas City Chiefs. Activists insist it is an insult to a proud heritage. My question is this: Where were they when the team was named in 1963 after moving from Dallas, Texas, to Kansas City, Missouri? Did they raise a fuss in 1963, 1964, 1965 . . . ? You see where I'm going with this.

Oh, and by the way, there is now a movement afoot to rename The Washington Redskins, the REDSKINS! And it is backed by Native American groups. You just can't make this stuff up.

Should you dare to venture to the *LibLand* city of Berkeley, Kalifornia, be prepared to have your common sense assaulted. Here is an absurd example of a city council taking political correctness too far—way too far. On June 16, 2019, the Berkeley City Council voted to ban gender-exclusive words such as *manhole*. Lord knows what underground utility workers are supposed to call those holes covered with fifty-pound steel plates!

What Berkeley needs is more police, not more idiotic politicians placating liberals for a living.

Random thoughts

I generally consider myself a solution-oriented fellow. So when I saw an article that Florida has a Burmese python problem, I swept into mental action and started searching for solutions. Note: We don't have a Florida python problem; it is a Burmese python problem. That means the snakes did not originate here—someone physically brought them here. And yes, they certainly have been flourishing. Hence the problem.

So I thought of Governor DeSantis's playbook with the illegal alien problem and noticed his rather unique solution. He physically rounded them up and took them somewhere else. Light bulb!

The governor could have his folks round up the offending pythons and ship them to Democratic strongholds such as Kamala Harris's grandiose home, Elizabeth Warren's mansion, or Nancy Pelosi's gated fortress. Alternatively, he can just truck them to New York City, Chicago, or San Francisco. I'm sure the pythons could find plenty of illegals to feast on. Perhaps the illegals will start heading south of the border—a win-win situation. Problem solved . . .

NOTABLE AND QUOTABLE

The country will survive Obama, but it cannot
survive the abject ignorance that elected him.

—Rush Limbaugh

Of particular interest to the communists is the
influence of fellow travelers and sympathizers in
the "thought-molding" field: teachers, script writers,
newspapermen, news analysts. If these individuals can
be subjected to the slightest bit of communist thought
control, the Party will have won a major victory.

—J. Edgar Hoover

MEMO # 25

Political doublespeak with a dash of horseshit

He knows a thing or two

Larry Kudlow served from 2018 to 2021 as the Director of the National Economic Council during the Trump Administration, so he knows a thing or two about economics. Listening to him in the media, I hear him discuss topics such as unlimited welfare state, rising taxes, massive deficits, high inflation, big government Socialism. From Bernie Sanders to Elizabeth Warren to President Biden, these politicians are comfortable with such things while I join Mr. Kudlow in his disgust.

Over-regulation on steroids

Word has it that the Biden Administration is after more than your gas stoves. You can expect the climate police to come after your refrigerator and dishwasher, and washing machine, too.

I've long been aware that Democrats are prone to push more regulations to stifle business, intrude on citizens' private lives, and create obstacles for families to overcome. Don't be surprised if they come after your driveways, swimming pools, front doors, and bidets!

Holy moly, Batman! There's a new federal acronym that escaped my notice! Does anyone know what WOTUS is? Why would you? The geniuses have trouble saying the "Waters of the United States," and now they say WOTUS . . .

The U.S. Senate is not a CCRC

The United States Senate is one of the two houses of the Legislative Branch. A CCRC is a continuing care retirement community. The two should not be confused.

Prior to her death in September 2023, Senator Dianne Feinstein (D-CA) announced her retirement and said she would not seek reelection. That is a good thing since the senator was eighty-nine years old and suffered from diminished mental capacity. Just hours after Ms. Feinstein announced her retirement to the media, she told a group of reporters that she had not yet decided if she would retire.

She held on to her Senate seat for thirty years. **The liberal folks in Kalifornia just kept reelecting her.** While Kalifornians can say *Thank you for your service, Senator,* it was clearly time for her to step aside and get the help she needed. What's worse is that Senate leadership allowed her to remain in her position and vote on important issues while knowing she could not reasonably understand what she was voting on. Thank you, Senator Schumer.

This is yet another reason why I am a staunch believer in term limits for both the House and the Senate. The founders never intended senators or members of the House of Representatives to make it a full-time, multi-decade-long career.

Department of doublespeak

Back in February of 2023, the Biden Administration made headlines when they announced the sale of 26 million barrels of oil from the Strategic Petroleum Reserve.

The Department of Energy explains the rationale for selling additional oil from our emergency reserves for non-emergency political reasons:

The Department of Energy (DOE) said in a statement announcing the sale, "The Administration is focused on replenishing the SPR in a way that provides the best deal for taxpayers by aiming to repurchase crude at a lower price than it was sold for, while providing certainty to the industry in a way that helps encourage near-term production."

DOE is looking to replenish the SPR over the long term through direct repurchases with revenues obtained through emergency sales, exchange returns that include a premium to volume delivered, and legislative solutions that avoid unnecessary sales unrelated to supply disruptions—such as through the arrangement included in the recent omnibus.[34]

My take: Political doublespeak with a dash of horseshit, a pinch of you gotta be kidding me, and a tablespoon of your mother would wash your mouth out with soap for being a lying bureaucrat.

The severity of economic damage and destruction of our energy independence inflicted by the Biden Administration is incalculable, yet Progressive Democrats insist that President Trump was the one who caused tremendous economic harm and damage to our energy infrastructure. Evidently facts do not matter more than ideology.

Yep, Kalifornia lunacy all over again

It's no secret that Kalifornia is pushing renewables and electric cars. Their politicians openly favor the demise of the internal combustion engine, and the dismantling of oil and gas pipelines, as well as outlawing gas ranges in your kitchen. They want everything electric. One problem though, their electrical grid seems not to be up to the task.

Under the weight of electric everything, the grid may fail big-time.

So here is my rather childlike, unscientific observation: *If Kalifornia's grid is facing collapse, is that due to faulty, flawed, incoherent, idiotic, and incompetent leadership of the Democratic majority that has been in charge of making the rules and calling the shots in the state for decades?* Can they honestly find some other entity other than themselves to blame? After all, it wasn't the French, the Germans, the North Koreans, or Trump. Governor Hair-Gel Newsom will never point the finger at the state's leadership, but who else could be at fault?

Random thoughts

There is only one national anthem. It is the one you learned in school as a kid. Every morning at P.S. 40, we stood and recited the *Pledge of Allegiance*, and at school assembly every Monday, we sang the National Anthem. There weren't alternative anthems for Jews, Christians, Asians, or African Americans. There was ONE—and it applied to all Americans no matter the color of their skin or where your grandparents came from.

The number of stories written about one of the least effective members of Congress should give you pause. Ask yourself this: Why would the media—you know, those ostensibly unbiased bastions of reporting accuracy—write and print story after story on Ms. Cortez, the New York Democratic Socialist whose claim to fame, to my knowledge, is never having a bill she authored ever, ever, ever make it out of committee, any committee, and whose effectiveness in Congress places her at the bottom of the barrel.

Yet almost daily, every media outlet splashes her picture and headlines about her, saying anything just so Americans can see her face over and over again, hoping that repetition will pave the way for an eventual seat in the U.S. Senate. I hope I'm wrong and that we don't see an America led by AOC and Britney Spears. Who else but organizations intent on bringing America to its knees would promote Social Democrats as if they were our saviors?

It's no surprise that Biden's budget focuses on raising taxes for corporations and *the rich* to bring down the deficit. Far be it from me to suggest the Biden Administration focus on spending less instead of taxing more.

They don't get it

Have you ever wondered if gun-free zones work? Some cities, including NYC, have designated certain areas as gun-free zones and erected signs informing their citizens. My question is, do criminals look up at the signs, and if they do, do they obey them? If I had a few minutes more while sitting in my dentist's waiting room, I probably would have learned that New York City politicians don't get it that green signs affixed to lampposts don't deter violent criminals who are intent on harming people. Guys, these are the same folks who don't get gun licenses or buy their firearms at Costco or Walmart. Criminals don't read signs. Law-abiding citizens read them. How collectively stupid can you all be?

Biden's policies have hurt the middle class

In the course of writing this book, I reviewed over twenty articles discussing the pain that Bidenomics has wrought to the middle class. Due to the unchecked spending policies of the Biden Administration, inflation soared to forty-year highs, mortgage rates doubled since Donald Trump left office, and prices at the pump for both gas and diesel are significantly higher since Mr. Biden took office.

I don't have to remind you that the costs of chicken, beef, eggs, milk, and other grocery products have soared and that consumers are paying lots more dollars for the same bag of groceries. Broken supply chains caused building materials to soar, if you can even get them. Yet through it all, *the Teflon administration* has blamed every problem on someone else. They tell us that the farmers are gouging us, the energy companies are gouging us, the builders are gouging us, and of course, it is President Trump's fault. The easy money policies of the Biden Administration caused runaway inflation, and to solve the problem, the Federal Reserve Bank raised short-term interest rates month after month, causing mortgage rates to nearly double and the worst U.S. bond market in forty years. If you have a home equity line of credit (HELOC), chances are your interest rate has skyrocketed.

The middle class would do well to open their eyes and ask whose policies have benefited their country, their neighbors, and their families: Mr. Biden or Mr. Trump? And if they're not sure, I invite them to ask the Americans who live on our southern border who have to live day after day with the disaster at our border, the unchecked illegal immigration, and movement of tons of fentanyl and other drugs to our communities.

For what it's worth, the Trump I support is an extremely knowledgeable problem solver, strong leader, and crisis manager, who posses a greater understanding of leadership principles, economics, and foreign policy than his opponents. Everyone who runs for president is flawed; we all are. We don't elect our leaders based on a popularity contest, or on who is the most handsome or appealing. We elect them based on whether they can do the job better than the next person. Period.

Hold on to your wallets

Long ago, my dad shared with me that keeping money is way harder than making money. I didn't understand it at the time, but I was reminded of his warning when I started to see articles about confiscatory taxes being discussed in state capitals. The inoffensive term given this idea? Annual wealth taxes.

In their never-ending strategy to tax every dollar that is not nailed down, some states, among them California, are trying to push bills that would tax wealth above $50 million. If you have $50 million, they seek to confiscate 1 percent annually, and if you have $250 million, they seek to confiscate 2 percent annually. If you're worth a billion or more, don't even ask, just pack your bags. After all, the states are on a mission to redistribute wealth and *pull up* those folks who don't like to work for a living, put an electric car in every garage and a vegan meatloaf in every electric non-gas operated oven.

An intelligent strategy to counter a state that proposes an annual wealth tax, such as one that California is proposing, is to leave, simply uproot and move across state lines. You don't have to have a $50-million or higher net worth, you just have to be fed up with insanely-high and unjustified state taxation. California in particular is notorious for figuring out new ways to fleece folks of their hard-earned money. They take *pay your fair share* to a whole new level. It's not enough to tax your income, now they want to tax net worth—the wealth successful individuals have built up over a lifetime. Tell me this does not smack of *Atlas Shrugged* and the warnings author Ayn Rand wrote about over sixty years ago.

NOTABLE AND QUOTABLE

Why is it inflationary if the people keep their own money, and spend it the way they want to, [but] not inflationary if the government takes it and spends it the way it wants to?

— Ronald Reagan, President of the United States

We don't have a trillion-dollar debt because we haven't taxed enough; we have a trillion-dollar debt because we spend too much.

— Ronald Reagan, President of the United States

MEMO # 26

Media insists on choosing HOT imagery to describe politics

**There's artificial intelligence (AI)
but there's no artificial wisdom.**

—Parthiv Shah

Trump did it! While playing golf

I was annoyed and amused, but not surprised to learn that after the 2023 Ohio train derailment and subsequent wreck, that Secretary of Transportation Buttigieg managed to blame it on Donald Trump. I have no doubt that Biden Administration officials will always find a way to blame Trump for everything. I would surmise that during the latest train derailment, Mr. Trump was most likely on the eighteenth hole of one of his golf courses. But of course, he is still to blame! Amazing . . .

Intro to Bidenomics

Bidenomics = spend it, tax it, regulate it

This is Econ101 for the Biden Administration. As long as everything his administration is doing abides by these three rules, they run with it.

- They spend money the United States does not have.

- They want to increase taxes on darn near everything.

- They want to regulate everything from your land use, the puddles in your driveway, your stove, your refrigerator, your washing machine, and more.

And don't forget, a byproduct of Bidenomics is something the Federal Reserve Bank likes to call *monetary tightening*. If you think it's like tightening your belt, think again.

It is the process of increasing short-term interest rates to make credit less available.

Midyear 2023 saw the average interest rate on a new car loan between 6 percent and 7 percent, and for used cars, approximately 10 percent. Mortgage rates are hovering between 7 percent and 8 percent, depending on credit scores. Bidenomics has proven a horrid strategy for tens of millions of Americans.

Just what we need—another recycled Obama bureaucrat

Again, I was dismayed but not surprised after reading a dated but accurate article published in a December 22, 2020 *Newsweek* article[35] by Katherine Fung where she made us all aware that almost 60 percent of Presidents Biden's cabinet choices are recycled Obama officials.

It certainly looks like an Obama reunion to me! Lord knows what the number is today.

Media insists on choosing HOT imagery to describe politics

Not a day goes by without the media describing interactions among Democrats and Republicans in the following manner:

- Senator scorched for comments on . . .
- Congressman shredded for tweet about . . .
- Administration official blasted for remarks on . . .
- Talk show host torched Presidential candidate . . .
- Big-city mayor roasted after allowing . . .
- Cabinet member vilified for decision to . . .

Hey, folks, do you see a common theme here? It appears that civility in the media is no longer a consideration. Do normal people actually speak like this? What would Walter Cronkite think?

Senators—Why don't YOU put your money where your mouths are?

Filings with Securities Exchange Commission (SEC) show that Elon Musk donated Tesla shares worth almost $2 billion to charity in 2022.

So, while Elizabeth Warren, Chuck Schumer, Bernie Sanders, Nancy Pelosi, and company rail against *the rich* and how evil they are, here we have a billionaire poster child donating almost $2 billion to charity in one year. Senators, why not give it a rest?

By the way, Mr. Musk is a signatory to the *Giving Pledge*[36]—a commitment by some billionaires to give away at least half their wealth. And hey, why not visit the *Giving Pledge* website and see the scores of billionaires who have pledged over half their wealth to charity. Hey Nancy, Elizabeth, Chuck, and Bernie—why not take the pledge???

The only good billionaire is a JAILED billionaire!

How's that, Joe?

I was actually a fan of the Biden Administrations Made-in-America EV Charging Network, until I learned that his administration waived the *Buy America* rules. Biden mentioned the made-in-America nationwide EV charging network in his State of the Union Address and ended with this: "I mean it!"

Heavy-handed state regulations

If you live in Minnesota, the days where you are permitted to use gas-powered lawn mowers and chainsaws might be coming to an end. All this to stave off climate pollution and the end of the world as Minnesota elected officials see it. Former Energy Secretary Rick Perry is right. This is about controlling your life—gas stoves, washing machines, lawn mowers, chainsaws. Where does it stop?

Have you heard that the D.C. government believes that an $80,000 annual income is a low-income household in the District of Columbia? If $80,000 a year is low-income, I have a bridge in Brooklyn I would love to sell you! Yes, they want to replace gas stoves for free if new legislation becomes law.

The D.C. government is hot to replace death-causing gas stoves for free, but at the same time they want to lessen penalties for carjacking and other violent crimes. The useless D.C. City Council is hell-bent on driving out law-abiding, taxpaying citizens and leaving the city with a pile of illegal aliens and criminals. Just marvelous!

Let me make something abundantly clear: There is no such thing as free. When a government chooses to provide a segment of the population with free stuff, the free stuff was paid for with taxpayer dollars. In other words, the government cannot give to one without taking from the other.

Economy landing in question

"Uh, United heavy flight 434, this is Kennedy tower. You are cleared to land, runway seventeen right. I repeat, you are cleared to land, runway seventeen right." See? That wasn't so hard. The flight is *cleared to land.* The runway? *Seventeen right.* Fact and fact—no room for challenge or misinterpretation. Not so with economic forecasting.

The New York Times, the *Wall Street Journal, Forbes, Fortune, Reuters,* and more—I have read articles addressing "the upcoming recession" until my eyes are ready to bleed. Soft landing, hard landing, and now a major update from *a major money center bank*—no landing! It certainly seems like there is no shortage of opinions, even while all these journalists and economists pour over the same data—the same facts.

Will the economy experience a hard landing? (Definition of hard landing: an economy swiftly shifting the spectrum from growth to slow growth to no growth as it approaches a recession, often caused by government actions to slow down inflation.)

- Will the Fed go on an extended camping trip and admit they don't know what they're doing?

- Will the Bureau of Labor Statistics suddenly publish data that everyone can agree on?

- Will Jamie Dimon, J.P. Morgan Chase Bank's CEO, admit he doesn't know how this will play out?

Stay tuned as we help poke fun at the experts and, like you, attempt to figure out if we are in a recession now or if the recession is starting in the second quarter, the third quarter, or at year end—or maybe in eighteen months!

It kind of reminds me of the sex psychologist who knows 275 sexual positions and can't get a date on Saturday night!

NOTABLE AND QUOTABLE

Good for you, you have a heart, you can be a liberal.
Now, couple your heart with your brain, and you can be a
Conservative.

—Glenn Beck

If our nation is ever taken over,
it will be taken over from within.

—James Madison, fourth President of the United States,
Father of the Constitution

Liberals measure compassion by how many people are
given welfare. Conservatives measure compassion by
how many people no longer need it.

—Rush Limbaugh

As an American I am not so shocked that Obama was
given the Nobel Peace Prize without any accomplishments to his name, America gave him the White House
based on the same credentials.

—Newt Gingrich, former Congressman and Speaker of the House

MEMO # 27

San Francisco's morality police shoots itself in the foot

Sometimes I just have to stop and notice how many ideas coming out of Washington reflect the stupidity of our elected politicians. But I don't want to poke fun at the feds only, the states have their fair share of lunatics as well.

I love Texas—but NOT this Texas

Let me take you back to the dark days of 2020 when the "defund the police" movement lit up every front page from Denver to Oakland, from Seattle to New York City, from Minneapolis to Baltimore. After the unfortunate death of career criminal George Floyd, city councils across the nation voted to slash police budgets and redirect funds to social programs, completely unaware and sometimes unwilling to consider the consequences of their actions.

Remember when local politicians in Minneapolis hired armed guards for personal protection because local police payrolls were threadbare due to mass resignations of active-duty police who refused to work for a government that did not respect them?

Well, in Austin, Texas, street racers took over a major intersection, partiedwith massive amounts of fireworks, and created a seriously dangerous situation. In fact, police were injured, and police cars were damaged in the ensuing violence.

What the media chose to focus on for headline shock value was an Austin City Council member who was on hold with the 911 emergency call center for twenty-eight minutes, trying to report the unfolding chaos.

It seems like council members are now concerned about police vacancies. Stop for a moment, and ask yourself some questions:

- Would you take a job that required you to work on weekends?

- Would you take a job that had mandatory overtime requirements?

- Would you take a job that pays less than other jurisdictions in the same state?

Don't let me forget Oregon's stupidity

Help me to understand why young boys need to be protected by the Oregon State Government enacting "The Menstruating Equity Act," which requires free tampon machines in both boys' as well as girls' restrooms. To add stupidity on top of irrationality, the official language of the act terms the children as "menstruating persons."

So, while this country is dealing with unprecedented crime, hate, massive illegal immigration, a fentanyl crisis, a debt crisis, raging inflation, high gas prices, high interest rates, and more, Oregon politicians remain some of the stupidest in the country.

There is no Constitutional right to work from home

A number of companies are mandating that employees get their asses back to the office. Apple let it be known that employees are expected to be in the office three days a week. Other companies are making it clear that if you do not wish to be in the office, you best find a new job.

Morgan Stanley, my old employer, was a bit more direct. James Gorman said at an investing conference, "If you can go to a restaurant in New York City, you can come into the office. And we want you in the office."

Workers became used to Zoom calls in their bedrooms, dressed only in their underwear. Many don't realize that you don't climb the corporate ladder in your pajamas. Success is often measured by burning the midnight oil so that your boss can see you in your office behind your desk.

Of course, you could always settle for a career with Door Dash delivering pizza, wings, and fries.

Stupidity is costly and ineffective

Here it is again—stupidity at the local level. Peel away the famous early-morning San Francisco fog, and consider the following:

San Francisco politicians made the decision that the city would restrict business and contracts with Conservative states that did not share their views on gay rights and abortion rights legislation. All was well until city officials realized they had shot themselves in the foot. My understanding is that contracting costs actually increased as the city banned more and more states from receiving San Francisco government contracts. Evidently, the well-intentioned city council did not understand the consequences of their actions. An excellent read on the subject can be found by reading Ashley Carnahan's article on Fox News reported on February 19, 2023.[37]

Nice job, San Francisco! You're wasting citizens' money once again. I'm sure your taxpayers are elated at your fiscal behavior. When will you learn that there are consequences to your actions?

To quote Forrest Gump: "Stupid is as stupid does"

I'm sure TSA personnel manning airport security stations across the nation find all sorts of interesting items in carry-on luggage, including cocaine, ivory elephant tusks, sex toys, weapons of all kinds, and more. But congrats to the New Orleans airport TSA folks for stopping a dangerous idiot from boarding a Texas-bound flight on February 14, 2023, with a fully loaded automatic weapon along with five additional magazines totaling 163 rounds of ammunition.

According to the TSA, the fellow faces a fine of $15,000—which I view as too little punishment. How about minimum mandatory jail time of forty-eight months and a fine of $25,000 for being a dangerous, stupid idiot?

Treatment is in the eye of the beholder

While driving home recently, I stopped at a red light and looked around at the stores on my left and right. I spied a sign that read, Medical Marijuana Treatment Center. For just a moment, my mind focused on the word treatment.

By now, many of you are probably familiar with how my mind works. I started considering what treatments would be prescribed for what ailments. Here is what I came up with:

- How ya doin'? Well, I feel like crap. What ya got for me? Well, we have some Columbian Tiger Weed or perhaps some Hawaiian sensamelia.

- Fellow comes in with lower-back discomfort. What can you give me for my back? Well, how about some Guatemalan Trainwreck or something a little less powerful like California Godfather?

- Good afternoon! Thought you might like to know that this week we're having a special on Jack the Ripper and Hulkberry if you're experiencing retrograde ejaculations.

So, my friends, beware when you see the word treatment 'cause you never know what might happen next . . .

NOTABLE AND QUOTABLE

**In the end, this world will go under
because of the stupidity of people.**

—George Harrison, Beatle extraordinaire

MEMO # 28

There are stupid Democrats in Florida too

There are stupid Democrats in Florida too

Did you hear the one about a Democratic Florida lawmaker who wants to make it illegal in the state for a dog to stick its head out a car window? Check out Senate Bill 932[38] that would ban dogs from sticking their heads out the window to enjoy a breeze. The bill was introduced by State Senator Lauren Book, who obviously has nothing more important to work on. Anyone care to consider the penalties this genius has in mind?

Are Chicagoans smart enough to place their mayor on the political trash heap?

You don't have to be a rational conservative to understand that Lori Lightfoot, Mayor of Chicago, is a jackass. I bet even misguided liberal Democrats on Lakeshore Drive might be wondering if their choice of mayor wasn't the best decision they ever made. Under Lightfoot's reign, Chicago has become the murder capital and cesspool of the Midwest.

Seeing her pictures in the media made the bile rise in my throat, and yet I stopped and read the headline. I'm glad I did. It seems she again was trying to worm herself out of a hissy fit when **she**

told voters who don't support her to not vote. Then she claimed she "misspoke." Funny thing . . . when I looked up synonyms for misspeak, I found the following: deceive, con, betray, delude, and my favorite—dupe.

It seems Her Honor has been duping, deceiving, and deluding the fine folks of Chicago for some time now. The smartest thing they can do is vote this jackass out of office and tell her to ring a bell on the way out so they know she is gone. Chicago, it's time to take out the garbage.

UPDATE: Lightfoot lost the election only to be replaced by another political hack.

I knew I liked this guy

I received a money pitch in the mail from Florida Senator Marco Rubio. In it, he relates that I have been at the top of his mind. Well! Now I have to read it. He goes on to say what he's focusing on—things that are very meaningful to me (and his millions of other constituents). One thing he said caught my eye, and I liked it. "I introduced legislation to ban TikTok nationwide, so we block Communist China from spying on us and manipulating public opinion with an algorithm they control." I liked that, and I can get behind it. Sorry if any of you are addicted to cute baby and kitten videos. Find another site!

Seattle's about-face

If all you did was read the news, you would discover many cities reversing "defund the police" policies as crime rates soar. Politicians are now discovering they have a huge crisis on their hands, and it is their fault.

Seattle, like Chicago, Denver, LA, Minneapolis, New York, and other cities, learned their lesson the hard way. The only thing that keeps the animals at bay is a strong sheriff and the rule of law.

So if the adults are let back in the room and the entire city council is fired, perhaps new city management will plead with now-retired law enforcement professionals to come back. Maybe those officers will see a new attitude and a deep, abiding respect for the work they do. And maybe they will have reasonable workplace rules and a generous pay package.

Elon peeled back the onion, and what did he find?

Much has been written about Elon Musk's purchase of the online behemoth Twitter. I will not opine on the new transparency, which I gleefully support, or the firing of all those who would burn down the village we call America while deleting posts that liberal supervisors viewed as offensive. Rather, I have become very aware of the prolific trickery, deception, and dishonesty that permeate the online world.

Make no mistake, the online world is still the Wild, Wild West. Laws that apply to brick-and-mortar businesses often do not apply to online businesses. The giant online corporations—Google, Facebook, Instagram, Twitter, and others—all rely on the number of users and active accounts in order to entice advertisers and buyers of media to purchase their online real estate. Was Elon stunned when he discovered that millions of accounts were fabricated or closed? Was he lied to when he reviewed the company's books that reported so many accounts? I'm not the smartest cookie in the jar, but I can tell ya, the more he peeled the onion back, the more rot he found. It will be interesting to see how the company transforms under his leadership. Stay tuned.

Bring your sleeping bag to the bank

Reports out of Lagos, Nigeria indicate that the country is facing a cash shortage. Folks are camping out and sleeping on bank doorsteps to be first at the ATM when it's restocked in the morning. Yet another reason to hoard your cash. Don't think it can't happen here, especially with the jackasses in charge.

Beatles fact

In the 1970s, astronomer Carl Sagan wanted to include the Beatles' song "Here Comes the Sun" on the Voyager's Golden Record. The record was launched into space as a message for potential extraterrestrial life. While the former band members were unanimously in favor of including the song, their recording company, EMI, nixed the idea.

This is a tough choice

America is starving for great leadership. I think we can agree that a great leader can be defined as one who has excellent character and exceptional experience. President Biden has neither of those traits. His leadership is . . . well . . . there is none. Also, I have grave doubts as to his mental ability to fulfill the obligations of the office of the President of The United States.

The Republican nominee for president in the 2024 race is anybody's guess, but the party will have to be solidly behind one name and one name only if they have a chance to beat the liberal Democratic ticket. But it appears that we may have three interesting contenders—Trump, DeSantis, and Haley. Each of these candidates possesses the qualities to galvanize and lead this country to a better future.

Only one has the in-your-face experience, and that is Trump. Ron DeSantis has done a marvelous job governing Florida, and I like and respect him even though he graduated from Harvard Law. Nikki Haley has a tremendous intellect, is a phenomenal speaker, and is as sharp as a whip. Let's see how this unfolds, shall we?

YES! The President is fine, please hold, yes, the President is fine, please hold

Here's a raise—now do your job

Have you heard that the Internal Revenue Service has managed to improve their customer service? By the way, the customers? That's us. We are called taxpayers.

Apparently, the agency is answering nearly 90 percent of taxpayer calls, up from 13 percent during the 2021 and 2022 tax seasons. I for one would like to know what John and Jane Jones, working as customer service reps for the IRS, were doing while they weren't answering over 85 percent of the calls that came in.

Okay, quick review. Government agency—check. Customer service reps, JOB is to answer phones—check. The reason for the insane jump in answered calls is due to new funding. So it comes down to this: If we give you more money, you will do the job you were hired to do! Insanity like this exists nowhere but in the government!

NOTABLE AND QUOTABLE

If a political party does not have its foundation in the determination to advance a cause that is right and that is moral, then it is not a political party; it is merely a conspiracy to seize power.

—Dwight D. Eisenhower, thirty-fourth President of the United States

"In June 1957, Nikita Khrushchev, Soviet Communist Party boss, was interviewed before a nationwide American television audience. With calm assurance, he stated: ". . . I can prophesy that your grandchildren in America will live under Socialism. And please do not be afraid of that. Your grandchildren will not understand how their grandparents did not understand the progressive nature of a Socialist society."

—J. Edgar Hoover, First Director of the FBI

"The present state of the world, the political events, proposals, and ideas of today are so grotesquely irrational that neither I nor any other novelist could ever put them into fiction: no one would believe them. A novelist could not get away with it; only a politician might imagine that he can".

—Check Your Premises, Is Atlas Shrugging? By Ayn Rand, The Objectivist Newsletter, Volume 3, number 8—August 1964

MEMO # 29

Yank their teaching licenses and boot them out the door

Will gender warriors ignite a California construction boom?

In the early part of 2023, California Democrats were embroiled in discussions regarding the idea of mandating gender-neutral bathrooms for all public schools' kindergarten to twelfth grade.

The idea was that the bill would require all schools in California to have at least one gender-neutral bathroom. Safe to say, the largest state in the union has well over 25,000 public schools. Pardon the pun, but that's a crap-load of new bathroom redesign and construction.

So, pardon my stupidity, but if there are sixty-eight genders, as many liberal thought leaders insist, must there not be one bathroom for each of the sixty-eight genders? Perhaps this will start a construction boom in the Golden State as large, new buildings will be erected to house all the new bathrooms! Let's see . . . sixty-eight genders minus the two I know about leaves sixty-six. Multiply that by at least 25,000, and you get a mind-numbing 1,650,000 new bathrooms! Imagine how many jobs will be created—for only union workers, of course! Imagine! The salvation of KALIFORNIA is in the toilets! Seems fitting…

Another reason I don't like them

It seems that Bank of America, like its rival, those stagecoach fellas, can't keep out of trouble, stay in their lane, operate within the letter and spirit of the law, draw inside the lines, or behave. According to a Fox Business article by Ken Martin on February 24, 2023, [39] Bank of America—you know, the preeminent bank with the word *America* in it—well, the penalties assessed against them in 2022 topped $1.2 billion. That includes settlements as well as fines.

Now let's stop for just a moment and consider this. Over a billion dollars in fines? These folks not only violated the law once or twice but made a habit of it day in and day out. Instead of penalizing the shareholders—you know, all the mutual funds in everybody's 401(k) plans that hold shares of BAC—why not strip management of all their stock options and throw their collectives asses in jail? That would send a realistic and valuable lesson that this type of behavior will not be tolerated.

By the way

Congrats to the Ohio pizzeria advertisement for non-stupid people to apply for a job.

And . . .

Beware of wearing expensive Apple headphones in New York City since roving gangs on mopeds speed up behind folks and rip them off their heads.

And . . .

I dare you to engage a millennial in a conversation about work ethic and not want to tear their head off.

Would Russia ever be pushed this far?

Even if you like scary movies, you might be unprepared for Russian television. Russian State TV has aired discussions about nuclear strikes on both the San Andreas fault and the Yellowstone caldera (super volcano).

If Russian subs were to fire nuclear warheads from hiding spots in the Pacific Ocean, America might be consumed by fires and earthquakes that would doom our nation.

Do you think for a minute we would hear this trash talk bravado if Trump was in the White House? Personally, I doubt it. Russia has become more brazen in mostly all things since Sleepy Joe Biden arrived at 1600 Pennsylvania Avenue.

Measure twice, cut once

It's not often I venture to European news, as we have no shortage of lunatics serving in government. Yet, I couldn't miss stories about Spanish officials quitting because they approved train designs that were too wide for some train tunnels. I came away thinking that hundreds of millions of dollars of waste is a bit much to cover up in a monthly update to the boss. Way too big to dance your way out of. Had they asked, I have a spare tape measure, and I would have been happy to bring it along on a Spanish vacation. Just shows there are idiots working in government positions all over the world.

Fire these teachers!

It's no secret that many Washington State teachers would like nothing more than to withhold and hide vital information from kid's parents. Some go so far as to label parents *Christo-Fascists*. Were I a superintendent of schools, I would root out these teachers and work to bar them for life from teaching minors. They are not employed to aid and abet bewildered and vulnerable minors from important life decisions without their parents' knowledge. To call parents Christo-Fascists is beyond deplorable. How could the State of Washington condone this type of behavior from their teachers? Yank their teaching licenses and boot them out the door.

American Socialist paradise

Some time ago I wrote of a disturbing trend that has permeated our society—personal responsibility and work ethic have been replaced by sloth, five-hour workdays, conference calls from Starbucks, or Zoom calls in pajama bottoms, shirt, and tie.

It appears that a significant portion of the population is content to work as a Door Dash messenger or Uber driver, forsaking success orientation and wealth-building, satisfied with subsistence living and sinking to a level just enough to live on with the hope of continuing government handouts. Said plainly, *skating* has become a way of life.

At the same time, we are forced to contend with a government that is hell-bent on destroying our economy and turning the country into a Socialist paradise complete with government ownership of banks, means of production, and increased regulations—including outlawing gas stoves, gasoline-powered lawnmowers, gas furnaces, chainsaws, and gas-powered cars. Next will be outlawing washing machines, banks refusing loans to non-green-energy companies, and every aspect of government infused with diversity and equity inclusion mandates.

Missing patients alert

I had a very realistic dream. It went something like this: It appears that St. Elizabeth's Hospital (formerly known as the Government Hospital for the Insane) has managed to misplace some of its most prized criminally insane inmates. Should you come across any of the following crazy patients, please contact your local law enforcement immediately. The missing patients are:

- Jerry Nadler
- Chuck Schumer
- Nancy Pelosi
- Maxine Waters
- Adam Schiff
- Alexandria Ocasio-Cortez
- Hakeem Jeffries
- Bernie Sanders

NOTABLE AND QUOTABLE

Your job here at E.F. Hutton is to get shit done. Get it done or you're outta here.

—Dick "Czar" Cardozo, my first boss at E.F. Hutton HQ in 1980

MEMO # 30

The government has lost touch with reality

You learn success from experts—not assistant professors at community colleges

I have a friend who is a great believer in self-education. He has been successful in numerous businesses, not because he is a college graduate (he isn't) but because he took time to educate himself on subjects that were important to him. He had to learn how to sell and how to market, so he took marketing courses taught by those who had real-life, in-your-face experience, folks who had made millions from their marketing and sales acumen. Those are the subject matter experts he chose to learn from. An assistant professor of marketing at the local community college would have been as valuable as a pimple on a college freshman's face.

Today, my friend owns a vineyard that produces thousands of cases of great wines. He is also the founder and president of several other businesses. He would be the first to tell you that sitting in freshman English class or Intro to Psych or Sociology is not the path to wealth. If you want to live your life on a college campus, perhaps that's where you should be. If you want to become wealthy, you should study wealth, study sales, study marketing, and study people. Left-leaning professors are not the path to the education you are seeking.

The government has lost touch with reality

The Creating Helpful Incentives to Produce Semiconductors (CHIPS) Act of 2022 is a $53 billion abomination designed to bring semiconductor manufacturing back to the United States. It's a worthwhile endeavor—but the devil is in the details, and in this case, the devil is an *out-of-its-mind* federal government. In order to qualify for funding under the CHIPS Act, a company must pledge to provide childcare for its workers with a facility at the factory to house little ones while mom or dad works.

While we're at it, if the Chicago Police Department gets federal funding, why not require them to construct a playpen—right next to where they lock up the drug dealers, carjackers, and prostitutes? *The White House and the Democrats in Congress have lost touch with reality.* The purpose of the bill is to ensure America has a robust supply of high-technology semiconductors that are not manufactured by hostile powers. This is about the security of the country—not liberals' desire to provide free daycare.

I admit it—I fell off the wagon

I was doing so well, limiting myself to just a few a day—but then those ugly Democratic harebrained headlines caught my eye, and I started monitoring the media like I was a drunk who fell into a vat of Jack Daniels. I was doing so well on my *media diet*, limiting the amount of online media I was viewing. But as I see it, it is entertaining, although my blood pressure most likely inches up a few points when I read of Elizabeth Warren and her economic rubbish or of AOC wanting to disband the U.S. Customs and Border Protection (CBP).

I never expected the unexpected

My road to informing and entertaining you in this book was not a straight, expected, or simple path. Rather, it came together through a number of unlikely circumstances such as sending emails to friends and family about what pissed me off that day. It came by reading too many headlines about the dire course our country is on; the non-stop transformation of our constitutional republic into a Socialist trash heap; the WOKISM of our schools, universities, and military; and the absolutely horrific job liberal Democrats are doing in the Senate and White House.

In 2020, I did not expect America to take a sharp curve off the rails and head into a ravine, courtesy of idiotic voters intent on voting for the candidate promising the biggest chicken to fill their empty pot. I didn't foresee direct Treasury payments going on long past any sensible pandemic-related need. I didn't see all the senseless students rallying the government to cancel the student debt they freely agreed to. In many cases, they now find that courses they took in the history of non-binary dance theory don't make them an attractive candidate in the job market where employers are looking for actual skills.

Did any conservative person who votes, stays out of jail, pays their taxes on time, and constantly seeks to do the right thing ever expect a set of circumstances that we as a nation now face? And I forgot to mention the forty-year-high inflation, the doubling of mortgage interest rates, the high gasoline prices, and near-historic prices of diesel fuel.

You can't have it both ways Mr. President

Undoubtedly you have read about President Biden's contempt for the energy industry. Even an energy novice would realize that you don't pump a million more barrels of oil by pressing a button, even a big-ass button.

Increases in production are the result of long-term strategies meticulously planned and executed while facing every kind of local, state, and federal obstacle placed in its path. Yet the president expects—no, demands—oil companies to pump more oil and stop gouging customers at the pump. Little does he understand that Exxon, Chevron, Occidental, and other oil giants DO NOT CONTROL the price of oil. The global oil market controls the price.

Worse yet, Biden wants more domestic oil while he tells the oil giants that he wants to put them out of business in ten years. Hell, it takes ten years for many projects to mature to the point where the first barrel of oil is sent down a pipeline to a refinery. These massive projects run into the hundreds of millions or billions of dollars of invested capital—and the president doesn't understand one word of it. Yet he is okay begging Iran, OPEC, Saudi Arabia, Venezuela, and others to send us more oil instead of taking the handcuffs off our gigantic domestic energy reserves.

Where do you stand on welfare for the professional class?

A nauseating headline, right? Why on earth would professionals be entitled to welfare? Let's say it another way. If I attended college and knowingly went into debt with my eyes wide open so I could reap the benefit (what benefit?) of being a college graduate, why should I get a free ride at taxpayers' expense when President Biden waves his magic wand and proclaims, *Bippity boppity boop, your student loan debt is gone!*

Thankfully, the Supreme Court weighed in and said, *Not so fast, Joe!*

Those with student loan debt do not fall under the Heroes Act passed by Congress. This is a horrific example of executive power gone wild. If you have a master's degree and can't repay your debts, it's best you work as an Uber driver part-time. I'm a hard working taxpayer, and I'm not here to bail you out

Deal with China from a position of strength

President Trump has made it exceedingly clear how he would deal with the massive trade imbalance with China. If reelected, his new trade policy would eliminate China's most favored nation trade status and ban federal contracts for companies that outsource to China. Personally, I think this is a brilliant and ballsy move. President Biden lacks the character to deal from a position of strength—it's not in his DNA.

Evidently there is A LIST—and I'm at the top of it

Wow! First, Senator Marco Rubio and now presidential contender Nikki Haley are sending me letters that say, *You're at the top of my list.* Evidently, I stand out among their most loyal friends. Who knew?

I'm certain I will be hearing from my governor very soon, and most likely I will be at the top of his list too! Perhaps they are all using the same copywriter to write their letters. Or maybe it's a kind of top-of-the-list groupthink. Now I have to figure out who I will support. But I'll be damned if we will have four more years of Biden's idiotic policies.

Fox News makes kids dumb in math

I wrote previously about the horrific state of Baltimore's public schools and their poor showing in standardized tests and math. What is new is that a Democratic jackass, Maryland delegate Sandy Rosenberg, is now blaming the poor showing on Fox News. Yes, you read that right. A media organization is responsible for thousands of kids failing miserably at math! That's proof positive that another Democrat should seek new employment, perhaps in a copper mine. And hey, I'll gladly buy that delegate a shovel.

NOTABLE AND QUOTABLE

I'd rather be right than be president.

—Henry Clay, Senator from Kentucky (1831)

I apprehend no danger to our country from a foreign foe. Our destruction, should it come at all, will be from another quarter. From the inattention of the people to the concerns of their government, from their carelessness and negligence, I must confess that I do apprehend some danger. I fear that they may place too implicit a confidence in their public servants and fail properly to scrutinize their conduct; that in this way they may be made the dupes of designing men and become the instruments of their own undoing. Make them intelligent, and they will be vigilant; give them the means of detecting the wrong, and they will apply the remedy.

—Daniel Webster, fourteenth and nineteenth
United States Secretary of State

MEMO # 31

The politics of blame

Okay, where do we have to go to get a crane around here?

It's come to my attention that we have a problem. Actually, we have a bucketful of problems, but I will focus on President Biden's *Buy America* initiative. You see, it's all roses and lilies to talk about a manufacturing renaissance and blue-collar jobs by the millions, but as I love to say, the devil is in the details—something the Feds never consider.

As we think about the massive infrastructure bill that became law—you know, the one showering hundreds of millions, hell, billions of dollars on ports, dams, green energy, roads and bridges—it seems the USA no longer manufactures many of the items needed to improve our dams, port, bridges, and such.

That is the problem from a 40,000-foot view. Now let's get up and in your face. You know how I feel about Transportation Secretary *Buttcrack*. He would serve the world in a much better way as a coal miner or a barista with shiny shoes. Well, apparently U.S. ports are in need of electric dock cranes, so they requested a waiver because **those type of cranes are not manufactured anywhere in this country.** The genius Secretary vetoed the request to purchase imported dock cranes. So, the port authorities are left in *Never Never Land* between federal mandates and an idiot cabinet Secretary. You can't make this stuff up. Another reason why this incompetent should be impeached.

The politics of blame

You want to win a quick five bucks? Show me a mainstream daily media such as *The New York Times*, the *Washington Post*, the *New York Daily News*, the *Post*, *Fox*, the *Wall Street Journal*, or *Newsmax* that doesn't post a story where a politician blames an opponent, someone from another party, a past president (that's one of my favorites) for one thing or another, and I'll personally send you five bucks. *The politics of blame* is rampant on both sides of the aisle and in every branch of government—federal, state, and local. Teflon Joe blames everything on Trump, Russia, or the evil Republicans.

I get it. Some blame is warranted, but most is merely an attempt to deflect the truth and pursue an untrue narrative to convince folks that they are really not seeing what they are seeing. If you tell a lie enough times, people will believe it—due to sheer repetition.

Here's a prime example. Biden insists that the more than $7 billion of arms left *in the country* during the chaotic withdrawal from Afghanistan cannot be used by the Taliban because fleeing American troops smashed control panels in Black Hawk helicopters and other advanced weaponry. Well, Joe, what about the 250,000 automatic weapons and over a million mortar rounds? Those puppies don't require specialized maintenance and technical support. Miraculously, Biden blamed Trump.

Lest we forget, Chicago Mayor Lightfoot was voted out of office because Chicago became **crime central** where folks were afraid to walk their dogs at noon on sunny days. She blamed race and gender for her stunning loss at the polls. Had this gay African American woman done her job properly and focused on law and order, her voters would have gladly voted her another term, regardless of her sexuality, race, or gender.

And one other *notable high-profile blame*—NYC Mayor Adams says the removal of public school prayers caused a huge increase in guns in schools. That is no less harebrained than Baltimore public schools blaming Fox News for poor standardized test scores.

The blame game has metastasized like an out-of-control cancer affecting this nation's government and cities in ways I would never have imagined years ago.

Take my car, please

It appears that New Orleans has seen carjackings skyrocket, and residents are being warned not to sit in their cars. As I read this, I thought to myself, well, you normally do sit in a car, especially when you're driving. I guess your car should remain empty (without someone in it) so the carjackers have an easier job of it. Perhaps city residents should keep their car doors unlocked and the keys sitting on the seat!

A social and economic disaster

In case you missed it, America's labor participation rate is nothing to write home about. Seems there are a lot of folks who are not working because they don't want to. How they are eating is beyond me. Perhaps it is because mom is too generous. I venture that a lot of young folks are returning to their parents' homes.

So, all parents who have offspring living in their basements—eyes glued to their phones for nine hours, delivering Door Dash meals for another five hours, and sleeping ten hours. Might be time for some tough love . . .

I can walk a mile from my home and count over one hundred stores with "Help Wanted" signs in their windows. I highly doubt that your local businesses are different than mine.

Disturbing and then some

I was stunned by a headline I read on Fox News on March 3, 2023. It read: "Arizona School Board Member Says District Should Reject Hiring Teachers with Christian Values: 'Not . . . Safe'." [40]

It doesn't take a PhD to recognize that I call out brain-dead opinions and values. I often attempt to peel back the onion on their character and motives. After reading this, I asked Ms. Google for some examples of *Christian values*—not trusting my memory to recall them accurately. Here is a sampling of the values that this idiot is so against:

- Don't be a hypocrite
- Be humble
- Be generous with time and money
- Live a moral life
- Be honest
- Be kind to everyone

This is an example of the mindset of the kind of person allowed on this Arizona school board. I'm shocked that the good folks of Arizona have allowed deranged human trash like this to permeate and represent their communities.

Fear of optimism

The media go out of their way to warn that a sunny day is a prelude to global warming. As long as progressive liberal Democrats control the narrative, we will continue to see illogical headlines and storylines. As an entrepreneur who has built a practice from **zero revenues,** who has worked without a safety net for four decades, I can attest that without faith in the future we may as well be throwing rocks at each other and hiding in caves, fearing the end of the world with each thunderstorm, tornado, or earthquake.

Collectively, the media are intent on presenting the evils of a constitutional republic, capitalism, and freedom of speech—pushing the population to the idea that Democratic Socialism, whatever that is, is a good thing, much more humane than the present system that tolerates massive financial inequality. They fail to understand history where Vladimir Lenin espoused that Socialism is the transitory path to communism. *Think of Socialism as Communism with training wheels.*

NOTABLE & QUOTABLE

**The man who does not read has no advantage
over the man who cannot read.**

—Mark Twain

**We should be eternally vigilant against attempts to
check the expression of opinions that we loathe.**

—Oliver Wendell Holmes Jr., U.S. Supreme
Court justice from 1902 to 1932

MEMO # 32

Liberals voted them in—now have at it

Equal opportunity—not equal outcome

Yes, I annoy some of the people some of the time. There are many who are jealous of what others may have attained and view it as unfair that some might have more than they do. This country was founded on the belief of equal opportunity, not equal outcome. If I work seventy hours a week and am able to buy a Mercedes Maybach, you don't get to ride in it, much less own it because you chose to stay home with a PlayStation and watch Netflix. Certain behaviors lead to certain outcomes—it ain't rocket science!

I would wager that decisions made and behaviors followed differ drastically, and that was the main reason for different outcomes. It's not who your parents are, where you grew up, or what degrees you have. I've met Harvard grads who did not impress me. By the way, I went to a state college in the frozen armpit of upper nowhere.

Mind you, I'm NOT giving investment advice, but . . .

You think you get weird stuff in your email inbox? Well, we all do. I'm inundated with charitable requests as well as political fundraising mail. But one letter stands out because it certainly deserves the *how did you arrive at that?* award. In big bold letters out the top of the page it read:

If China were to cut us off now, the U.S. military would run out of minerals needed to make most weapons within a year.

—Supposedly said by Senator Tom Cotton

So naturally I thought it was a seven-page letter convincing me to give money to a political campaign. Wrong. Here's the pitch that followed:

This $6 stock is our best shot at defeating China . . . and it could soar as high as 8,990%. Okay, at least two questions come to mind. First, how is buying a cheap stock going to defeat China? And as if that weren't enough, HOW did they arrive at a potential gain of 8,990 percent on your invested dollars? And, why not just round it off to 9,000 percent. Would that be dishonest?

Liberals voted them in—now have at it

- Southern border disaster
- Millions of illegal aliens allowed in the country
- Eight percent mortgages—that's double, folks
- Taxpayer-funded student loan debacle
- The worst bond market in forty-one years
- Sky-high diesel gasoline prices
- Energy insecurity
- Massive increases in the cost of living (inflation)

According to CNN, the national average for regular gas on the last day President Trump was in office in January 2020 was $2.393 per gallon. Now, unless you live in Kalifornia, you're paying a buck higher.

How does this equal that, Janet?

JanetYellen, our esteemed US Secretary of the Treasury, is on record having said that eliminating women's access to abortion would have "very damaging effects" on the US economy and increase inflation.[41] I'm sure that as an economist she has come up with some very convoluted logic to support her premise.

I've heard that *abortion is an industry*, with many specialists involved, from doctors to nurses, to clinics, hospitals, to sanitation and cleaning companies, and more. I suppose that restricting access to abortions might have some kind of effect that would ripple through the economy. But I come back to the issue of scale. The "abortion industry" is not the steel, auto, or oil and gas industry.

When the UAW (The United Auto Workers Union) goes on strike, idling plants at Ford and GM, the consequences on our economy are tangible, measured in the billions of dollars. Economists and media talking heads show charts on the devastating impact on GDP (gross domestic product—the total of all goods and services sold in the U.S.) and the economy as a whole. Vendors, suppliers, restaurants and manufacturers of every kind are affected by the length of the strike, and often find themselves squeezed for cash as expenses continue but cash receipts drop off a cliff.

I just don't equate restricting access to abortions based on how far along a pregnancy is or if the mother's life is in danger would have a dramatic effect on our economy. I have a hard time connecting the dots—*how does this equal that, Janet?*

Swarthmore College discovers a new way to separate people

Mind you, the following new words added to our lexicon would have Miriam Webster spinning like a turbine in her grave.

On March 4, 2023, Eric Utter, writer for *American Thinker*, wrote about something that turned my head . . . twice. He wrote:

> *Pennsylvania's Swarthmore College proudly maintains—and regularly updates—a webpage cataloging the LGBTQ+ terminology it fosters and recognizes "BIQTPOC," Masculine of Center," and "Transmisogynoir" are among the terms and phrases the school sanctions. Really.*
>
> *According to Swarthmore, "Transmisogynoir refers to "cultural and interpersonal systems of oppression affecting and against Black, transgender women," whereas "Masculine of Center" is a "gender identity label for a queer person, typically assigned female at birth but not always, who presents masculinely; most often utilized by queer women of Color." Alrighty, then. And "BIQTPOC," which the esteemed institution of higher learning definitively says should be pronounced "bye cutie pock," is an acronym for "Black and Indigenous Queer and Transgender People of Color."[42]*

In case there is any question, the Swarthmore administration has lost its collective mind.

Should you decide to send your child to the college, you are most likley in desperate need of therapy.

China threatens our way of life and our politicians back legalized marijuana

I can't be the only person who recognizes that while China is arming itself to the teeth building warships, submarines, fighters, and bombers at breakneck speed, politicians across America, particularly liberal Democratic ones, are feverishly pushing for the legalization of marijuana for recreational purposes.

It might be interesting to note **that marijuana is illegal in China**, except for industrial purposes (hemp, etc.). While China's leaders are ensuring their populace is not stoned, they are, in fact, running their factories seven days a week, out-producing America in practically everything. Does this not smack of a disaster in the making?

Democratic members of Congress, as well as state legislators from blue states, are determined to allow their entire states' populations to light up and be happy. While they possess the legislative authority to do that, I don't recognize their moral authority to pass such ludicrous laws.

Meanwhile, our labor participation rate is abysmal while around the world the Chinese are back at work post-COVID out-producing us by mind-numbing amounts. Wrestle with that idea and see if you can come up with a bright side to that.

I think back to my college days when dorms were regularly searched for drugs. If any found, they were confiscated—students were scared that campus security would refer their findings to local police and parents. Today, we have Senators and Congresspeople cheering for pot and smiling while asking for your vote. Meanwhile, China locks stoners in jail and fines them to boot. Who else thinks this situation is insane?

And lest we forget, the next time you bring your car in for new brakes or fly anywhere, remember that the mechanics keep a *travel bong* or loose joints in their car for a quick hit of pot on their way to work. Think about the airline people who worked on the oxygen mask system above your head or the mechanic who worked on the elevator you took to the seventeenth floor. Yeah, all these folks may get a quick hit of pot on their way to work. Hey, it's legal! So how does that make you feel? Safe and happy? Paranoid?

Or consider a conversation in the break room at a major (unnamed) car manufacturer where three stoned production line workers are searching for their rolling paper so they can light up one last joint before completing their shift. Ever wonder why Ford, GM, Tesla, Toyota, and others are incapable of producing a car that doesn't have to be recalled for SAFETY problems?

NOTABLE AND QUOTABLE

The most important thing to do if you find yourself in a hole is to stop digging.

—Warren Buffett

There are more instances of the abridgment of the freedom of the people by gradual and silent encroachments of those in power than by violent and sudden usurpations.

—James Madison, author of the United States Bill of Rights, fourth President of the United States of America.

MEMO # 33

Spinning BS: Biden thinks a
31 percent tax increase is modest

Unreasoned and thoughtless nonsense

If you've read this far, you are probably aware that I spend a fair amount of time reading. To form intelligent opinions, you need to *suck up* a lot of information from diverse sources, let it percolate for a time, and then form opinions based on data and thought.

Unfortunately, I see many around me spewing forth unreasoned and thoughtless nonsense, hoping no one will stop to consider if their statements are misrepresentations or outright lies. Such is the case with statements coming from many Socialist Democrats—the extreme far left liberals who favor defacing the statues of our founding fathers, trashing the Constitution, and changing our nation's history to match their warped vision of the world. Make no mistake; these folks are as dangerous to the American way of life as Russia is to Ukraine, as Mainland China is to Taiwan, as Iran is to Israel.

And make no mistake; Ben Franklin's line, "A Republic if you can keep it," is as important today as it was when he exited the Constitutional Convention in 1787.

Equality alert

There will be no more *White Christmas* since it has been deemed racist. Henceforth, it will be described in all places and all things as "a frozen precipitation Christmas event."

Way to go, Oklahoma!

I feel compelled to congratulate them as they abide by the motto, *get stuff done*—and I have found that folks who get stoned all the time don't get a whole lotta stuff done! So, it was with a smile on my face that I read this headline: "Oklahoma Votes Down Recreational Marijuana."

Spinning BS: Biden thinks a 31 percent tax increase is modest

I came across the following headline, and I stopped to consider the math involved: "Biden Asks Wealthy to Pay 'Little Bit More' in Taxes to Avoid Medicare Insolvency" (Cami Mondeau, Washington Examiner, March 7, 202342).[43]

As part of his budget plan, Biden proposes to "modestly" increase the Medicare tax rate for taxpayers earning an annual income of more than $400,000, from 3.8 percent to 5 percent. My guess: he is considering the difference of 1.2 percentage points to be modest. (That's a 31.58 percent increase—do you call that modest?)

"Let's ask the wealthiest to pay just a little bit more of their fair share, to strengthen Medicare for everyone over the long term," Biden wrote in an op-ed to *The New York Times* on Tuesday, May 7, 2023.[44] "Let's ask them to pay their fair share so that the millions of workers who helped them build that wealth can retire with dignity and the Medicare they paid into."

Our country is spending hundreds of billions of dollars housing, feeding, clothing, and caring for illegal aliens who should never have been allowed in this country. Our taxes and deficits will keep rising as long as the government allows them to stay. I may be harsh, but they do not belong here and should be escorted across the border and out of this country as soon as possible. They are not our responsibility. Our responsibility is to Americans and all those who chose to come here legally and become part of the magnificent fabric of our country.

Every time politicians talk tax increase, they point to the wealthy paying their fair share—the ultimate UNDEFINED number. So, whatever you are paying now, you ain't payin' your fair share! The most successful among us are penalized for success with never-ending tax increases.

The federal government does not have a revenue problem . . . it has a spending problem.

It didn't take long

Scarcely forty-eight hours after the March 2023 collapse of Silicon Valley Bank, liberals came out in force, blaming the bank failure on Trump. Hey, why can't I get in on the game too? I'm overweight, and it's Trump's fault. I gave up trying to play the guitar when I was thirteen because I have NO ear for music and could not even tune my guitar, and . . . wait for it . . . it's Trump's fault! Gee! This game is fun. Let's all play.

- Chuck Schumer is incapable of telling the truth—it's Trump's fault.

- Nancy Pelosi is incapable of telling the truth—it's also Trump's fault.

- Kamala Harris is incapable of, well, anything—and it's Trump's fault.

Another reason not to go to New York City

Study: New York City Rats Carrying COVID-19

A new study found that rats in New York City are carrying COVID-19, and researchers have sounded the alarm that they could infect humans with it. Published Thursday, March 9, 2023, in the American Society for Microbiology's *mBio* journal,[45] scientists at the University of Missouri said they trapped seventy-nine rats from the city's sewer systems and found that thirteen had the virus previously, with four currently infected.

LGBTQ+ would love to rewrite the Declaration of Independence

Might their edits create the following?

We hold these Truths to be self-evident, *that all men, women, bisexuals, queer, transgender, cisgender, pansexual, gender queer, and non-binary* are created equal, that they are endowed by *nature* with certain unalienable Rights, that among these are Life, Liberty, a living wage, free medical care and free education and the Pursuit of Happiness. That to secure these Rights, *Governments are instituted among men, women, bisexuals, queer, cisgender, pansexual, gender queer, transgender, and non-binary*, deriving their just Powers from the Consent of the Governed . . .

Who knew?

Who was the man who doubled the size of the United States? President Thomas Jefferson purchased 830,000 square miles from France's Napoleon Bonaparte for $15 million in what became known as the Louisiana Purchase. Perhaps it was a better deal than the Manhattan purchase?

Who Should pay?

Here is a piece of a brilliant and very thoughtful essay by Nina May that appeared in *American Thinker* on March 12, 2023. The title of her article is "If We're Doing Reparations, Here's Who Should Pay Them." I recommend you read it all word for word.

"The Republican Party was founded in 1854 as an abolitionist party, with six of the nine planks in its platform dealing with abolishing slavery, equal rights, civil rights, and voting rights in the 13th, 14th, and 15th Amendments, respectively. The Democrats, on the other hand, had in their platforms in 1844, 1848, 1852, and 1856 that they proudly supported and defended slavery and the right of a person to own another person. They believed in it so strongly that when Abraham Lincoln, the first Republican ever elected, made it clear that he would rid the country of the scourge of slavery, the Democrats packed up their tents and seceded from the Union, causing a war that pitted citizens against each other, ending in almost 800,000 dead Americans.[46]

If one dime of reparations is paid to family members of slaves who suffered under the iron rod of a political party that fought a war to keep those slaves in bondage, it should be paid by the Democratic Party. Democrats not only left the United States of America but also formed their own country with their own president, currency, flag, constitution, elected officials, etc., etc."

Guess your elected Democrats don't like to talk about that…

NOTABLE AND QUOTABLE

**Independence means you decide
according to the law and the facts.**

—Stephen Breyer, Associate Justice of the Supreme Court

**The great thing in the world is not so much where
we stand, as in what direction we are moving.**

—Oliver Wendell Holmes, Associate Justice of the Supreme Court

MEMO # 34

Illegal aliens qualify for Medicare, Medicaid, and Social Security?

Sue their butts in court.

Judicial Watch is an organization (that I support) whose purpose is to call the government(s) out when they fail to play by the rules. Whether governments are ignoring federal law, the Constitution, or just being all-around jackasses, Judicial Watch does the research and then sues their butts in court.

I saw two articles in the Judicial Watch March 2023 newsletter that really struck a chord. Here is my take on what I read:

Victory #1

California Court of Appeals upheld an injunction against corporate board quotas. The political lunatics in charge of the state of California passed a law requiring certain corporations to have minimum quotas of sex, race, ethnicity, and LGBTQ. In other words, they needed two transsexuals, two lesbians, a guy with three testicles, an American Indian, an African American, and a white guy in order to satisfy the ruling political hacks. I'm happy that the California Court of Appeal sided with Judicial Watch and told California to *go pound sand.*

Victory # 2

New York City must clean up voter registration rolls and remove 441,083 ineligible names. The city is the home to some fiendishly devious political hacks when it comes to voting integrity. Seems that over the course of six years the City of New York removed only **twenty-two names** from their voter registration lists. Ya see, federal law states that reasonable steps must be taken by the states to clean up their voter registration lists.

New York City has over 5.5 million voters. And the folks in charge of election integrity removed only twenty-two people over six years. That is so shocking and disgraceful that I had to repeat it. Well, guess who sues their ass in federal court? You guessed it—Judicial Watch won a major victory (their words, not mine) when the city announced a settlement of the lawsuit and agreed to remove 441,083 ineligible voters. Hmm, twenty-two versus 441,083. Maybe someone should end up in jail? We can only hope.

Ya think some of them voted for AOC, Hochul, Schumer, and Biden?

Three cheers for 6 percent inflation!

On March 14, 2023, I read the latest inflation figures released by the government. It seems the CPI (Consumer Price Index) dropped to a **low** 6 percent inflation. Now, I know I am not living in a parallel dimension, and the laws of supply and demand, economics, and such still apply, but I ain't breaking out momma's good drinking whisky with a 6 percent number! Recall that under President Trump, the nation's inflation number was less than 2 percent, and thirty-year mortgage rates were 3 percent (they're now hovering at 8 percent).

Note to self

Hey, self! I can't recall seeing so many headlines of states suing the federal government and the Feds suing the states. Seems we are expending an incredible amount of time, energy, money, bickering, and fighting amongst ourselves instead of focusing on the ever-present threats from Russia, China, Iran, North Korea, and a host of other state actors. In other words, why aren't we forging ahead as a strong, unified nation? What this does is distract us from where we need to focus our efforts. Tell me this is a good thing, and I will smack you in the head with a bag of quarters.

Relentless stupidity

It seems that AOC is bitching about how difficult it is to make ends meet on her $174,000 Congressional salary. Yes, it's true that I am not a fan of Congresswoman Cortez. Still, you have to wonder how this young lady survives on her salary, which is three times the average American household. Oh yeah, and she drives around town in a Tesla. I really feel no pity.

We are all familiar with the sexy actress Sharon Stone who made headlines, not for a leading lady role in a new Hollywood smash hit but for sheer stupidity. Evidently, she admitted to the media that she lost half her money in the Silicon Valley Bank failure. A characteristic of relentless stupidity is not heeding warnings meant for human beings—such as don't feed the lions, sharks, or killer whales. By the way, killer whales come with an unusually explicit warning—they actually have the word *KILLER* in their name.

And if you are going to have a large sum of money, best you buy short-term Treasury Bills for liquidity (a direct obligation of the U.S. Treasury) rather than place the funds in a super-cool, super-woke regional bank. **Mind you, I am not giving investment advice here**, but Silicon Valley Bank is no J.P. Morgan Chase. Sharon Stone can act, but she's a financial dunce in a short dress—and there ain't nothing going on between her ears. Call it *the death of common sense...*

By the way, if you did something incredibly stupid, would you call the media and announce it to the world????

Aw, shucks! I'll give the money back!

Not one but two of my favorite political pinheads have agreed to relinquish political donations received from failed and famous SVB Bank. Apparently, both Chuck Schumer (D-NY) (Senate majority leader) and everyone's favorite insane California Representative, Maxine Waters (past ranking member of the House Financial Services Committee) will be returning financial donations received from Silicon Valley Bank's CEO Greg Becker.

And here's the lunacy—if I am a *Congressperson* and sit on a Congressional potato chip committee, it is incredible that I can continue to receive donations from potato chip companies and their executives! Hey folks, let's change the laws and vote these self-serving yahoos out of Congress!

Don't look now

DC Comics introduced *Bizarro World* in 1960. As a child (and as an adult), I read many a story where Superman was confounded by the imbecilic behavior of *Bizarro Superman* and the mayhem caused by a group of idiots who could not tell right from wrong, up from down, or east from west. Bizarro was a fictional planet where there was NO common sense—actually no sense at all. Everything was upside down and inside out. Hello meant goodbye, stealing was praised, pollution was good, and everything—including people's heads—were square. In fact, the planet was square!

So why do I bring this up? Surely you have noticed media headlines that defy common sense—or any sense at all—such as "Guess what Putin and Trump have in common?" How about arrest warrants out for both of them? Have you heard that North Korea has 800,000 volunteers who want to fight America? I don't recall us attacking them or wanting to claim any of their valuable resources—oh yeah, they have none.

What about tampon machines in boys' bathrooms in schools, or state laws allowing pre-pubescent gender reassignment surgery? Or how about defunding the police, the very people who protect us from those who would cause us harm? Why not defund the military at a time when Russia and China are endangering our way of life? Publicly funded abortion is not a human right. Or how about California deciding to give $5 million in reparations to African Americans who qualify? Mind you, California was never a slave state. *Diversity, inclusion, and equity* have gone mad in a modern-day Bizarro World.

Ask yourself this: What planet are we living on?

Don't worry, we are NOT the illegal aliens they are talking about

Medicare for all? Bah! Humbug! If far left Democrats had their way, every illegal alien would qualify for Medicare, Medicaid, and Social Security—effectively bankrupting our country. Open the gates, defund the customs and border protection folks, erase our borders so we become a failed state that once had so much potential. Venezuelans eat their zoo animals. Are we next? *Fentanyl for all.* Is this what America has come to? Understand that our country is at a tipping point. Wake up, America! There will be repercussions.

Boneheads and extremists such as Maxine Waters, Chuck Schumer, Adam Schiff, Gretchen Whitmer, Kathy Hochul, Joe Biden, Rashida Tlaib, Ilhan Omar, Kamala Harris, Bernie Sanders, Elizabeth Warren, AOC, and others are praised—much like in Bizarro World. The only difference is that **Superman**, my hero, is not here to save us. We must save ourselves, and we must start now.

NOTABLE AND QUOTABLE

I read somewhere that Biden's presidency is shaping up to be as bad as Jimmy Carter's. I think they are dead wrong—it is shaping up to be worse.

—Anonymous

MEMO # 35

The new *equity language guide* published by...

Pulling back the curtain

If you want to light your hair on fire, poke your eyes out with a salad fork, run naked across the twenty-yard line at the Super Bowl, or go for a blindfolded walk at the edge of the Grand Canyon, that is your right as an American. Of course, you will likely suffer the consequences such as jail, blindness, or death—but hey, it's your choice. All these moronic pastimes might be preferable to reading the new *Equity Language Guide*[47] published by the **Sierra Club**. You see, they have taken a commitment to equity, justice, and inclusion to a whole new level. The club is billed as an environmental organization whose focus is to *"defend everyone's right to a healthy world."*

Telling readers what words are bad and what words are good does not seem to support that objective. Kind of reminds me of George Carlin's *Seven Dirty Words You Couldn't Say on Radio*—you're a BAD WORD! By the way, as expected, they frown on the term *illegal alien* and would prefer the use of *"someone with a complex immigration status."*

This is clearly intended to be disingenuous and mislead people. An illegal alien is a person who **broke the law**, committed a **felony**, and

does not belong in this country. They have committed a criminal act and are a criminal. It is rather simple. There is nothing complex about it.

The next time you have a hankering to support environmental beauty, go plant a couple of trees, and think twice before giving this left-wing organization any of your hard-earned money.

An excellent article on this is on the *American Thinker* website. The story, written by Rajan Laad and appearing on March 23, 2023, is called "Another Self-Appointed Language Policeman Reports for Duty."[48]

Have you heard?

The liberal left is trying to erase the term pedophile from the English language. They are trying to replace it with *"minor-attracted person."*

One person is capable of . . .

At the very least, one person—note, I said person, not artichoke, not a three-testicle unicorn or gender number sixty-seven—is capable of influencing history, of bringing charm and smiles to generations of people around the world, being so known on the planet that everyone recognizes them by their first name, no last name necessary.

Case in point—a young fellow born in the United States put down a $1,000 deposit on a home. The date was March 19, 1957. The purchase price of the home was $102,500, which in 1957 was a king's ransom. The home became the second-most-visited home in America. It is known as *Graceland.* The young fellow . . . Elvis Presley.

Was he, as millennials call it now, an influencer? You bet! Elvis influenced millions around the planet—and kids from Cambodia to Toledo to Key West to the Bronx gyrated, played air guitars, and sang their hearts out to songs such as "Jailhouse Rock," "Blue Suede Shoes," "Love Me Tender"—and my personal favorite—"Viva Las

Vegas." In fact, my cousin Gary and I did a particularly God-awful rendition of "Viva Las Vegas" that would curl your toes and kill your eardrums. Were Gary and I influenced by Elvis? You bet your sweet ass we were.

Ask yourself this: How did Elvis influence and put smiles on the faces of tens of millions of people before the Internet, before TikTok, before YouTube, before Instagram, before Facebook, and before all the others? In a few words—talent and a burning desire. It was talent honed day by day, month by month year after year—a singular goal to be the best. And the world stood up and took notice.

Leave your pronouns at home

Should you wish to communicate with me my website is: EOCritic. com and my email address is: EOCritic@Protonmail.com

Be warned that **I tolerate no pronouns** before or after your name and will call you by whatever gender you were birthed as. If a surgeon named Rubeniwitz cut off your nuts and gave you girl stuff, keep it to yourself. Likewise, if you were born Sheila and now, through the miracle of surgery, you use the men's rooms and go by Big Jack, I ain't interested. Leave your pronouns at home.

Businesses will surely go under when working from home

Your brain would ooze out from your ears if I listed all the imbeciles I have dealt with in the past week—from big box stores to pool services to dishwasher repair. All customer service morons I spoke with were working from home—hence, they were unable to ask an office mate questions when answers eluded them. In every case, I was given bad information. Then I had to stay home and wait for delivery persons who never showed up—I seemingly was left off the schedule, or someone's Internet went down, and the business servers were not updated with correct information.

The excuses go on and on, and all have one thing in common—idiots in their underwear pretending to do the job they were hired to do while attending to their kids, washing their car, or sorting through the day's mail. Business owners have a choice—get employees' asses in their chairs, fire them, or bolt the doors and call it quits. If the current trend continues, folks like me who vote with their wallets will surely decide to take their business elsewhere—places where owners and managers police their employees and make certain they are where they are supposed to be and doing their jobs!

No tear shed

I lament the fact that many of my old friends never moved past their Democratic liberalism stage. They continue to live in blue states, vote the blue ticket from top to bottom, and mimic the old line that the rich don't pay their fair share. They are never ones to let facts get in their way. I have pared down to the bare minimum the amount of time I spend with them—just a "Hello, how are ya? And once they start in on the state of the world, I respond with, "Oops, I gotta go." There's only so much negative world view you could take before you have a craving to start smacking your head against the wall.

Only a Millennial would post this

I saw my first ad for a *Pinterest Strategist*. I didn't know that was a thing. As my mentor Dan Kennedy points out, different media are ALL MEDIA—doesn't matter if it's a message on a ballpoint pen, in the Yellow Pages, on a billboard, or at a bus shelter. But it might give me a giggle to read of a bus bench strategist or an ice scraper message strategist—and, of course, a Pinterest strategist.

Striking for a raise that would put most businesses OUT of business

I was not surprised when I read that teachers in Los Angeles, and other school union workers called for a strike. The schools were shut down. We have all seen this before. What caught my eye was their demand for a 30 percent salary increase Hey, why not demand 50 percent or 75 percent? Whatever happened to cost-of-living increases? In many careers, folks get 2 percent to 4 percent raises.

A 30 percent wage increase is a **huge** increase. When did insanity replace common sense?

Don't answer that. How many employers, no less a school district, can afford almost a one-third higher wage scale? If it was a private employer, say a Popeye's or Wendy's franchise owner, that would put them out of business. It will be interesting to follow the story. Many will call for higher taxes on the rich to pay for salary increases, while others will balk against higher taxes, and the mayor, city council, and governor will all be lashing out at each other for problems they alone created by their idiotic policies that span decades. Yet through it all, I remain confident that somehow, someone will blame it on Trump!

The gang that couldn't shoot straight

Characterizing the Biden Administration as *The Gang That Couldn't Shoot Straight* is a fair description of the inept leadership and the disingenuous and misleading information coming from our executive leadership. Name an area of the administration that is clearly providing thoughtful, clear, and pro-American leadership. Consider the following:

- Homeland Security Secretary Alejandro Mayorkas is insisting there is no border crisis and that we are in control of the southern border. His own people say the opposite, and the number of illegal aliens entering America is off the charts.

Worse yet, the secret airline flights that are resettling illegals via midnight flights to out-of-the-way airports are all orchestrated and condoned by the feds.

- Transportation Secretary Buttcrack took ten days to comment on the Norfolk Southern railroad derailment near East Palestine, Ohio, and then blamed it on President Trump.

- Vice President Kamala Harris has proved herself inept at everything and has no accomplishments whatsoever to show for her time in office. It seems that every time she opens her mouth, a shoe magically flies into it.

NOTABLE AND QUOTABLE

If you tell the truth, you don't have to remember anything

—Mark Twain

He's a beautiful man, but I'm sorry he doesn't agree with my political philosophy

—Tip O'Neill on Ronald Reagan

MEMO # 36

Is America better off under Democratic leadership?

Is America better off under Democratic leadership?

Stupefying might be an accurate term to describe the current batch of misguided politicians dominating the leadership of the Democratic Party. The inability to think and understand the consequences of their actions explains a lot. In my professional career as a financial advisor, I have crafted a number of quizzes for folks to take to gauge their views and progress on a variety of issues regarding financial planning, debt, cash flow, insurance, and so on. Today, I thought I would **surprise** you with a **pop quiz**. Don't worry, it's a fun quiz that won't be graded or shown to your parents. Its only purpose is to help you focus on what is truly happening *out there* and how it has gotten worse since Mr. Biden became president. I ask you to question everything, especially when the Biden Administration spins a negative into a positive.

Take this eleven-question quiz and determine for yourself if America is better off under the current Democratic leadership.

Do you have a **positive or negative view** of the following issues that have presented themselves under the current Biden Administration? For added fun, tally your answers, and make a list of Democrats you will no longer speak to.

1. Mortgage rates have doubled under the current administration.

2. Inflation has skyrocketed and become the number-one financial concern of most Americans.

3. Our southern border is in crisis mode with millions of illegal aliens flooding into our country due to the refusal of the administration to enforce immigration and border laws.

4. The administration has been secretly shipping and relocating illegal aliens into communities across the country without the communities' knowledge or approval.

5. Your elected leaders view themselves as blameless and not responsible for any of the current problems facing our country—blaming every problem on President Trump.

6. The nation's emergency Strategic Petroleum Reserve (SPR) is being drained and eviscerated for political purposes.

7. The administration is using strong-arm tactics, threatening to pull federal funding from school districts that do not buy into the Department of Education's plans for trans and gender-neutral bathroom facilities in all school districts.

8. The disgraceful, rushed, and poorly planned exit from Afghanistan left thirteen U.S. soldiers dead and billions of dollars of American weaponry in the hands of the Taliban.

9. White House spokesman John Kirby affirms that "LBGTQ+ rights are core to America's foreign policy"—thus solidifying

the Biden Administration's cultural standard that they are exporting these beliefs to other countries.

10. Interest rates have risen steeply, and Americans are forced to pay higher prices for everything they purchase on credit, from dishwashers to new cars to refrigerators.

11. America is perceived as weak due to the administration's feeble dialogue concerning bold moves from North Korea, Russia, and China—countries that seek to take advantage of our weak foreign policy.

By the way, don't ever get me started on continued supply chain issues and shortages.

A pronoun does not make a woman

Maybe I'm old school, but I would expect an award for *Woman of the Year* to be won by, well, a woman. We are witnessing more and more stories in the media about folks who were born and raised as Harold, Burt, or Johnny now insisting they are not the sex on their *original* birth certificate. They say they are women, parade themselves around in makeup and high heels, and bully those around them to address them with pronouns such as she and her, but they were probably all born with a prostate and a penis.

Case in point, a 2023 honoree, Minnesota State Rep. Leigh Finke, a man with pink hair who wears a dress and has been in elected office for about twelve weeks.

Famous people have a NEED to be in the news

Why else would a famous person admit to a sexual affair seventeen years ago when they were on the set of XXX? Because they feel it's necessary to be in the limelight, even if it's not flattering. Who cares what they did with their genitalia and who they did it with in 2006? Or who cares about J. K. Rowling's debate about what to call a rapist with or without a penis? Come on, folks!

Who cares what LeBron James thinks of a House bill that's being debated or what Harrison Ford thinks about pre-teen gender affirmation surgery? If they can't drink their coffee and pick up a newspaper and see their name in print, it's a bad day for them.

For many famous people, their lives are intricately intertwined with appearing in the media, and being spoken about at cocktail parties (yes, there still are cocktail parties, and the folks who attend them are often speaking of celebrities and their weird stories). They are not ready to fade into yesterday's news cycle and become someone who used to be spoken about. Perhaps they have an inability to *move on* and find other things that bring meaning to their lives.

The media plays along and continues to carry dozens of these stories daily. Should you meet a journalist, tell 'em that frankly you don't give a damn, and ask them why they don't stick to real news.

Bad decision in time

Let me take you back to that fateful day in February 1942. Joe Biden's dad makes the ill-fated decision not to wear a condom while having makeup sex with his wife, and eighty years later, look what we're stuck with!

A national divorce is OFF the table. Why? Because I said so!

As I look across our country, I often feel and THINK that reason has eluded us. Many think America has become an ideological war zone, and I can't say I disagree with them.

Groups from White moms, to Black moms, to Asian moms to

abortion rights groups, to radical climate groups, to anti-oil and gas groups, to pro-immigration groups, to far right and far left organizations, seems no one wants to talk or peacefully coexist with each other. America has become toxic, and we are all to blame.

The land mass of the Unites States is an astounding 3,531,905 square miles and it seems as if we are waging battles on every one of them. There is talk that *blue states* don't want to do business with, or even recognize *red states*. Folks, we are not getting a national divorce. We are one country with a hell of a pedigree. Should anyone you know forget that, I suggest you refresh them on American history, maybe gift them a copy of the Declaration of Independence or the Constitution. And while you're at it, suggest a trip to Washington, D.C. so they can visit each of the sacred monuments erected to the brave MEN and WOMEN of this nation who gave their lives so that their children, and their children's children could thrive in a free and great nation. They could also interact with the geniuses in Congress who helped get us into this mess while they are there.

The founders of America had an overriding ideal, and that was all of us living peacefully together in a free nation.

No gas in new buildings if the Democrats get their way

New York is hell-bent on regulating everything in sight. They have gone to great lengths to outlaw gas heat, gas stoves and other gas appliances in many classes of new buildings. Best those in the *formerly great state* of New York keep an eye on their legislators as single-family homes are next on their list.

With a Democratic mayor, governor, and legislature, they have a hell of a chance of all this lunacy becoming law. Forget for a moment that the majority of the citizens of the state are against it—another reason to never spend your hard-earned money in a state that does not value the opinions of their voters.

Why does his opinion matter (to anyone)?

I can't help but see the big TV bolted to the wall at my gym when I'm on the treadmill. I try not to look and be brow-beaten by the relentless media insanity. Yet on this fateful Sunday, none other than Howard Stern—perhaps the ugliest and least credible celebrity in the United States—was opining on President Trump's possible arrest. I don't know what channel was on, but why on earth would any news producer tell their crew, *"Go out and see what Howard Stern thinks about this."*

Yet another reason to tune out and turn off.

NOTABLE AND QUOTABLE

I think Kamala Harris is eminently qualified . . . to teach a third-grade elementary school class.

—Rodger A. Friedman

We are not educated well enough to perform the necessary act of intelligently selecting our leaders.

—Walter Cronkite

There is not such a cradle of democracy upon the earth as the Free Public Library, this republic of letters, where neither rank, office, nor wealth receives the slightest consideration.

—Andrew Carnegie

MEMO # 37

A wildly unimpressive Congressperson

Questions that SHOULD be asked

Did *mama Daniels* name her daughter Stormy, or did that nickname just catch on with her Johns . . . er . . . customers? Or perhaps *The Donald* gave her that nickname?

Before Republicans took back the House, wildly unimpressive Representative Maxine Waters (D-CA) chaired the House Financial Services Committee. Back in **2019**, the committee held hearings on the student loan mess. Madame Chairwoman was salivating at the thought of grilling and lambasting the CEOs assembled in the hearing room—CEOs of the nation's largest banks—and hit them squarely between the eyes, blaming the whole mess on them.

The Congresswoman spoke of large increases in the number of school loans and how over a million folks per year were in default on their student debt. Imagine this ill-informed idiot's surprise when she asked the first witness, the CEO of Bank of America, what he intended to do about it. "*We stopped making student loans in 2007 or so,*" CEO Brian Monahan replied. The CEO of Citigroup indicated that they had ceased making loans in **2009**. Jamie Dimon, CEO of JP Morgan Bank, had to school the chairwoman that when the federal government took over all student loans in **2010**, all banks got out of the business.

The question that SHOULD have been asked is why the American people tolerated this idiot as chairperson of the Finance Committee of the U.S. House of Representatives.

Yes, comrade, our thinking is properly leftist!

The *American Thinker* website had a fascinating article written by Ed Brodow on March 31, 2023, called "Diversity Executives: The U.S. Version of Soviet Political Commissars."[49]

I was blown away by some of the statistics and narratives such as, "Employing significant numbers of diversity executives is all the rage. The average university, for example, now has 45.1 people dedicated to promoting diversity on campus. The University of Michigan has a whopping 163 diversity officers." And here is the cherry on top: "Diversity, Equity, and Inclusion (DEI) executives—our political commissars —are tasked with enforcing leftist policies in corporations, universities, and government agencies. They do not contribute to the competent functioning of those institutions and in fact may detract from their profitability and efficiency."

Imagine that, your life is your fault

If you have the opportunity, you might wish to look up Candace Owens and the articles she writes. She is an excellent critical thinker and expresses her ideas clearly and intelligently.

I was very impressed with an article she wrote about taking full responsibility for the circumstances and outcomes in your life. I came away thinking that it is not the fault of your parents, your government, your next-door neighbor, or President Trump for your current situation. I particularly liked her ideas on responsibility and that too many of us are coddled and feel society should take care of us. It's a shame the mass media doesn't share her opinion. Were more folks to listen to her message and understand its importance, this country might not be spinning endlessly around the drain on the way to the sewer. Makes great reading on a rainy Sunday afternoon

Do seniors topple our nation's statues?

Do seniors topple our nation's statues, or are statues of Thomas Jefferson, George Washington, and even Abraham Lincoln toppled by disillusioned youth adhering to radical, false narratives of our nation's history? Those responsible seek to rewrite American history as a country founded on injustice and adhering to racist principles. Nothing could be further from the truth. If those responsible allowed themselves to be educated rather than persuaded by leftist ideologues seeking to overthrow the most notable democracy that exists anywhere, they would find a nation that is imperfect yet striving to be better, not the Socialist backwaters that dot the maps around the globe. These statue-topplers cling to Critical Race Theory (CRT) and push to have it taught in our schools. They subscribe to 1619 rather than 1776. They want to trash our history and replace it with state-sponsored racism.

Mike Pence, former vice president of the United States, is on record as stating that *"Critical Race Theory is nothing short of state-sponsored racism."* I agree. When was the last time you saw someone in their 60s or 70s—someone who raised a family, paid their taxes, worked for decades providing for those they loved, perhaps enjoying their grandkids—sneaking off to topple a statue of Thomas Jefferson?

Ask yourself, who is doing the toppling?

Media can't decide who's more important

As I write this, the media is jam-packed with articles about two people. One is President Donald Trump, who was recently indicted by a New York grand jury. The other is Gwyneth Paltrow, who has been the subject of a lawsuit.

Should you care to count the number of articles written about these two in mainstream media for a week, I'm fairly certain you would top 300.

I loved Paltrow in the *Iron Man—Avenger* movies. She played Tony Stark's sidekick and love interest. Skimming headlines only, I understand that Ms. Paltrow was sued because she was accused of skiing recklessly at a Utah resort and injuring someone. I don't care to learn any more than that. I'm busy. My point is that here is a Hollywood star who has appeared in dozens of movies and is undoubtedly worth hundreds of millions of dollars, and the media has turned the lawsuit into a daytime reality show reminiscent of the Jerry Springer mind-crap.

And consider this. If the ski accident in question was between a handyman and a fifth-grade teacher, it would barely rate a paragraph on page thirty-seven of the daily paper right under the legal notices. But the media loves to write about the travails of famous people with lots of money.

On the other hand, President Trump has also been mentioned in hundreds of articles as everyone and their grandmother weigh in on various aspects of the legal process, leftist New York DA politics, and everything from an assault on the Constitution to the House of Representatives' subpoena for the NY DA!

Time will tell who wins the media war of words, but I suspect that Mr. Trump will prevail.

Thoughts on entitlement

The word entitlement captures much of today's media opinion columns. They tell us that everyone is entitled to government paid housing, education, medical care, food, and even cell phones—not only for Americans but for illegal aliens as well.

Let me clarify so there is no possibility of a misunderstanding. YOU break the law, YOU enter this country without permission, YOU are a felon, and YOU believe YOU are entitled to free education, housing, medical care, food, and, YES, even a cell phone. My, what a big pair of brass balls YOU have! Better you are tossed in jail pending deportation.

NOTABLE AND QUOTABLE

You know why there's a Second Amendment?
In case the government fails to follow the first one.

—Rush Limbaugh

The democracy will cease to exist when you
take away from those who are willing to
work and give to those who would not.

—Thomas Jefferson

Memo #38

Economics: Uncle Warren versus Biden

Important question

Is the decline of America transitory?

Listen to Kevin

Want an earful? Catch economist Kevin Hassett as he discusses the intellectual bankruptcy of the entire Biden Administration as well as their lack of commitment to the truth. Hassett is former Chairman of the Council of Economic Advisors to President Donald Trump. I'm sure if you Google him, you will find his latest comments. He is someone worth reading and listening to.

Chicago is a scary place

Those wonderful folks living in Chicago have recently elected a new mayor—Brandon Johnson—**a leftist former union organizer and social studies teacher**. Senator Bernie Sanders and Senator Elizabeth Warren endorsed Mr. Johnson. Were I a Chicagoan, a better choice might have been a retired police chief to introduce a new concept to the city—Law and Order! Regardless, the progressive Democrats deserve what they voted for. Go Chicago!

Friends don't let friends vote Democrat.

Giggle me this Mr. President

Want a giggle? Ask Biden to explain modern monetary theory. Want to roll on the floor? Ask Biden to explain his new tax policy without mentioning that it's time for the wealthy *to pay their fair share.*

Riddle me this

It's mystifying that employment growth tends to be higher in the public sector than in the private sector—meaning more folks are getting jobs working for the government than in private industry. That is how Biden is growing the economy, by hiring more government workers. Am I the only one who has a problem with that?

Meanwhile, airlines are cutting the number of flights due to air traffic controller shortages.

What happens when the government floods the economy with easy money through reckless overspending policies? Simple. Read the headlines, check your 401(k), look out the window, and see the prices at your local grocery store. Your mind will grasp the answer real quick.

This is what happens when you listen to an idiot

Did you hear about a Davis County, Utah school board that is reviewing its *inappropriate content policy* as it pertains to school libraries? Evidently, an idiot complained about content found in the Holy Bible. My guess is the only time they cracked the book was to search for things they disagreed with. If I want to find things I disagree with, all I have to do is wake up each day and read a newspaper, or the online equivalent.

New York City is run by fools

Have you heard that New York City will no longer refer to public restrooms as *comfort stations* to avoid the pretext of any connection with the term "comfort women?" This term was common many years ago and described those forced into sexual slavery in Japan during World War II.

I'm sorry, but the deranged legislators who run NYC are wasting precious resources of time and money to distance them from something that happened in another country over 6,000 miles away more than half a century ago. Meanwhile, crime is rampant, citizens are unsafe on the streets in broad daylight, and you take your life in your hands when you ride the subway.

In case you missed it

It should be no news that Mr. Biden did ultimately blame Donald Trump for the chaotic Afghanistan withdrawal. Another fine example of the Teflon Administration. Nothing sticks to them, and they take no responsibility for any negative outcomes.

Surely you have read that those wonderful folks at NASA have hired a diversity ambassador. So, the next time there is a tragic failure of a space mission with loss of life and billions of dollars, remember that NASA felt they needed more equity, inclusion, and diversity rather than quadrupling the safety protocols.

Leave it to Los Angeles Councilman Curren Price, who proposed a bill calling for a $25 minimum hourly wage for tourism workers. I assume that the following workers would be included under the *tourism banner*:

- The guy (or platypus) that stands on the corner waving a sign announcing bus tours to movie stars' homes
- A county tour guide leading folks through Los Angeles parks

- The young lady (or artichoke) selling tickets to water taxi services

- A travel agent trainee

- A golf cart tour guide

- The ghost and haunted house tour guide

Why any of these career choices merits a $25 minimum hourly wage is beyond me.

You would think that a more intelligent way to raise living wages is to provide reasons for folks to gain greater expertise and be more valuable to their employers, thus earning—**yes, earning**—a higher wage. It seems that idea is lost on the councilman who, of course, is an attorney and a *professional* Democratic politician.

Please note: If my children grew up to be *professional Democratic politicians* I would take them out of my will and leave my money to charity.

Even if you don't live in New York, you must have heard that the esteemed Goldman Sachs has provided *pronoun pamphlets* to its employees so investment bankers and the like do not *misgender* a porcupine for an anteater. Were I a Goldman banker, I would bid *a cold day in hell goodbye* to management that has buckled to the woke ideology.

In case there was any doubt, YES, the sun will eventually destroy the Earth. It will burn off our atmosphere, making life on this planet impossible. But the bright side is that it will occur in about a billion years. So, if you have any to-dos on your to-do list, you best get at them. A billion years will be here before you know it. And if you were wondering, I'm pretty certain that progressive liberal Democrats will find a way to blame the Earth's demise on Donald Trump.

Central planning Socialists—top-down Socialist government

A casual reading of the United States Constitution makes no mention of the ever-expanding administrative powers of (Biden's) EPA. The agency is hell-bent on remaking industry after industry. They're after auto tail pipe emissions, and they're making a radical push for electric vehicles. The EPA wants to control fossil fuels, home appliances (stoves, refrigerators, gas furnaces and washing machines) and in your garage—gas-powered leaf blowers, and lawn mowers.

Economics: Uncle Warren vs. Biden

Much has been written about the Biden Administration's ever-evolving rules regarding corporate share buybacks. Space does not allow for a complete review and discussion of the strategy but suffice it to say that I view buybacks as an important financial tool used by many publicly listed companies.

Yet Joe Biden views them as a tool to enrich wealthy shareholders and corporate executives. Under Biden, buybacks are now subject to a 1 percent tax, and the government is attempting to raise it to 4 percent—all of this to put more money in U.S. Treasury coffers.

Interestingly enough, according to one of the most successful investors in American history—Warren Buffet, chairman of Berkshire Hathaway—his view is that:

The math isn't complicated. When you are told that all repurchases are harmful to shareholders or to the country, or particularly beneficial to CEO's, *you are listening to either an economic illiterate or a silver-tongued demagogue*—characters that are not mutually exclusive.

NOTABLE AND QUOTABLE

In America, year after year, we lose our best people but always seem to keep our worst.

—Christopher C. Miller, former Acting Secretary of
Defense under President Donald Trump

The truth has no defense against a fool determined to believe a lie.

—Anonymous

Small men, seeking great wealth or power, have too often and too long turned even the highest levels of public service into mere personal opportunity.

—Barry Goldwater, Air Force Major General, five-term
Senator from Arizona, Republican Party nominee
for president of the United States in 1964.

Patriotism is not a short and frenzied outburst of emotion but the tranquil and steady dedication of a lifetime.

—Adlai E. Stevenson, U.S. Ambassador to the United Nations,
Governor of Illinois, and Democratic nominee
for President of the United States

Memo #39

Who is responsible for the
dumbing down of America?

Great job, Ben

I'm a reader. In order to write this book I needed to gobble up a bunch of media online and offline—books, magazines, and even audio books. I require a lot of raw material to comment on. One goal is to read one to two books each week (an actual book made from trees and turned into paper). Let me share a superb read that might interest you.

A big shout-out to Ben Shapiro for a masterful job on his book *The Authoritarian Moment: How the Left Weaponized America's Institutions Against Dissent.*

Ben is an author, a graduate of Harvard Law School, and a native of California. He has since relocated to a sane state with more reasonable politicians and lower taxes. Many know him for *The Daily Caller* and *The Ben Shapiro Show.* He is considered by many to be one of the most influential and rational conservative voices in America today.

I recommend the book without reservation. It casts a well-considered view of how the left has infiltrated much of our country and the damage it continues to do to America.

I'll get my medications from your competitor, thank you very much

In case you missed it, CVS Pharmacy has issued a gender transition guide that states employees must use preferred pronouns and can use bathrooms reflecting identity. Additionally, employees may be entitled to medical leave of absence for gender transition treatment.

Why not just proclaim, *Only the woke shall survive*? One more reason why I am no longer a customer of that store and have switched my prescriptions to a competitor. I urge other rational conservative adults to do the same.

Rub two sticks together and get electrons

It seems Germany is now burning more coal than ever to generate electricity. Oddly enough, they have closed the last three of their nuclear plants because they say they are not green or sustainable, and yet the electricity has to come from somewhere. You don't rub two sticks together and get electrons. Their leaders had better figure out a way to heat their homes and power their factories that does not rely on coal. Although they produce a formidable amount of green energy, Germany's industrial production needs a huge amount of power to sustain their GDP and economic strength.

You could learn a thing or two from the bagel man

Bear with me as I revisit and update you on a new twist to New York City's almost 9 percent sandwich tax. Anyone living in NYC has no doubt seen an added 8.875 percent tax added to their sandwiches and even bagels with a shmear of cream cheese. No shmear saves you dough; a shmear takes money out of your pocket and gives it to the taxman.

Enter the entrepreneurial geniuses at H&H Bagels who got together with the Philly Cream Cheese folks to, in effect, circumvent the dreaded bagel tax. Follow this: their new bagel comes pre-loaded with crème cheese, no slicing, so shmearing, no nothing. Oh, and no added tax either!

I'm pretty certain that the New York City Council will call an emergency meeting to figure out how best to respond to this assault on their taxing authority.

Random thought

It saddens me to consider that America's best and brightest days may be in the past, not the future. What is sadder is that my children and their children will have to live in that world.

The stuff nightmares are made of

Imagine for a moment a new cast of characters heading powerful committees in the House and Senate—liberal, Socialist-leaning members who would strike fear into the hearts of Conservatives from Montana to North Dakota to Florida. AOC, Chairwoman of the powerful House Ways and Means Committee; Bernie Sanders, Chairman of the Senate Judiciary Committee; George Soros Jr., Chairman of the House Appropriations Committee; and last but not least, Madonna as Chair-something of the Senate Select Committee on Intelligence. And further, Madonna would be viewed as the voice of reason. Be scared. Be very scared.

Revisiting Kratom

Previously I have commented on many signs for businesses advertising Kratom. But now we've entered a whole new realm. I am seeing signage that says *Legit Kratom*. I guess that makes all the difference? And by the way, who is it that's saying it's legit?

Who is responsible for the dumbing down of America?

The most obvious place to begin is our public schools and colleges. Great numbers of kids who graduate from high school or college have never been exposed to the following skills:

- How to write a resume

- How to land a job

- Basic banking—checking and savings

- IRA accounts and employer-sponsored retirement plans (401(k) and 403(b))

- How to negotiate a lease for an apartment

- Personal development skills and goal achievement

- Fundamentals of success

- How to buy a car

- Comparison of trade school education versus college education

But our schools are not the only culprit. Look at online media. Whether I look at liberal or conservative media, much reporting is no longer done in words. They are videos. People no longer have a need to read when they can watch the news.

I remember when I was a kid, my dad would send me out on Sunday mornings for bagels and newspapers. The *Times* and *News* combined weight was about two and-a-half pounds, and my dad would spend a fair amount of time reading about local and world events. He was well-informed and well-read, something I can't rave about with today's younger folks.

There's no line for that on the bank deposit slip

I want to share a conversation I had with a musician who has fallen on hard times. Since COVID, the number of band bookings is but a fraction of what they were, and income is down by about a third. But rather than take advantage of the hundreds of help-wanted signs within ten miles of this musician's home, he would rather stay home and bitch about the drop in income. Mind you, he is no spring chicken, and a loss of one-third of his income is significant and painful. Now he has a list of things he must do without and things that must be postponed or made skinny by lack of past abundance.

Deposit slips accompanying band receipts were cool—call it musical cash. Deposits representing earnings from a restaurant, retail store, or any number of jobs that pay $15 plus per hour are not cool. Yet the bank deposit slip does not have a line for cool money, hard-earned or uncool money. It's all the same—green and in the bank. This musician would rather stay home and bitch about how bad things are. Little does he realize that the economy affecting him *is between his ears*, and his lack of motivation to get off his ass and earn more money is a personal decision, and a poor one at that.

I remember back in 1980–1981. Jimmy Carter was president, and his lack of any skills other than the Navy or peanut farming was evident to all. There was massive inflation, high gas prices, and out-of-control interest rates. And then there was me—nary a skill, I would gratefully clean floors, stock shelves, and sell anything and everything to put food on the table and keep a roof over my head. I was **entitled** to nothing, and I knew it. Nothing was below my dignity. I had to bootstrap it. My dignity was earned hour-by-hour, week-by-week, and paycheck-by-paycheck. My self-worth went up along with my self-esteem and bank account. Ego did not get in the way of cash earned.

NOTABLE AND QUOTABLE

They may hold positions of leadership, but they are not really leaders. They may be entrusted with great responsibility, but they never take responsibility when it really counts. Our ruling class is incapable of ruling. And they should not be trusted with America's future.

—Christopher C. Miller, former acting Secretary of Defense under President Donald Trump, former Special Forces Commander, and Green Beret

Unfortunately, the American people are saddled with an administration known for political doublespeak, a dash of horseshit, a pinch of you gotta be kidding me, and a tablespoon of your mother would wash your mouth out with soap for being a lying, two-faced bureaucrat.

—Rodger Friedman

A recession is when a neighbor loses his job. Depression is when you lose yours. And recovery is when Jimmy Carter loses his.

—Ronald Regan, fortieth President of the United States (Labor Day Address at Liberty State Park, Jersey City, New Jersey, on September 1, 1980)

Memo #40

Titans, AOC, and Gitmo

Tell me this is not stealing

A friend of mine out West shared the following story with me. He noticed the managers at his gym appeared very busy when the owner was on the premises. However, once the owner left, both the general manager and assistant manager sat at their desks glued to their phones, often for an hour or more. He has seen this repeat enough times to understand that *this is the way things are done around here.*

Please tell me the difference between stealing petty cash or office supplies and stealing an employer's time where tasks and functions that should be completed are not. Tell me this is not theft. And tell me that you would hire employees whose values tell them this is acceptable behavior. It is not. **Stealing has consequences**, something that liberal Democratic district attorneys may want to remember. This has everything to do with the character of the individual, not their race, sex, or who their parents are. Were they my employees, they would get one warning, and if the behavior persisted, they would be fired on the spot. They call it work for a reason.

The lightning bolt

Get ready to scribble. This is as much a part of my life as a good cup of coffee is part of my morning. It occurs often in my writing life and when I'm reading books or the daily paper. It happens even when I'm listening to an audio book. A "lightning bolt" sears across my brain, sending me off in search of a pen and paper to capture the idea for later use while it's still fresh with profound meaning and striking images. Keep a pad and pen handy, and capture your genius moments or grand idea.

Disingenuous behavior—you expect it from prison inmates, not the White House

If you have followed the 2023 debt ceiling controversy and how Speaker McCarthy and House Republicans seek to limit the growth of the federal deficit, you have undoubtedly noticed the responses from White House Press Secretary Karine Jean-Pierre when asked about Mr. Biden's views regarding GOP overtures to rein in federal spending. Several articles I read in April 2023 all indicated that the Speaker of the House has put forth several reasonable ideas, only to be summarily shot down by the White House. Among these ideas are the following:

- The bill would increase the country's borrowing limit by some $1.5 trillion through March 2024.

- It would roll back federal spending to 2022 levels.

- It would limit growth of the deficit to 1 percent annually.

Granted, there are other areas that will cause Democrats to lose their collective minds, such as repealing portions of the Income Reduction Act and work requirements for able-bodied individuals enrolled in federal assistance programs, among others.

But the disingenuous White House Press Secretary characterized these ideas like this:

- Increasing energy bills
- Cutting education, veterans' benefits, cancer research, meals on wheels, food safety, and law enforcement
- Killing good-paying jobs
- Forcing American manufacturing offshore
- Taking healthcare away from millions of Americans
- Protecting wealthy tax cheats
- Pushing tax giveaways to big corporations
- Raising taxes for hard-working families

Think for a minute and look at it this way: if I gave you a simple choice of a red or blue hard candy and you chose the red candy, here is what I believe the White House would say:

- You are a hater of blue candies
- You are a racist and fascist
- You want to put blue candy manufacturers out of business
- You want to put blue candy employees on the welfare line
- You want to gut healthcare benefits for blue candy employees
- You want to put blue candy employees in the poorhouse
- You are MAGA evil
- You are heartless
- You are what is wrong with this country

Worth the wait?

Walk through an airport concourse, and you may see something I've seen time and time again—a long, winding line of customers, heads down, cell phones in hand, waiting patiently for their turn to purchase a Starbucks coffee. Meanwhile, forty or so feet down the concourse is Dunkin' Donuts with two folks waiting in line. Remember, both these stores sell hot (and cold) brown water. Granted, Starbucks is known for adding many tasty ingredients that add sugar, calories, and pizzazz to their creations. But in the final analysis, is their coffee hotter, browner, or less watery? Just something to think about the next time you are eighteenth in line at Starbucks and I am already being served a steaming cup of hot coffee at Dunkin Donuts on the concourse.

Titans, AOC, and Gitmo

If you're familiar with the names Caitlyn Jenner and Dylan Mulvaney, you might have noticed media reports informing us of some kind of battle going on between them. Battle? Whether they carried swords and shields into a rumble, or a Rambo knife, I'm not sure. But what is at best puzzling, at worst inane, is that the media characterized these two as "trans titans." Come on now, surely the media has something better to write about without insulting our intelligence.

First, who anointed these twits *trans titans*—or titans at all? What the hell does it even mean? In the old Hollywood movies, titans had muscles on their muscles and defeated the bad guy, armies, demons, evil kings, witches, and sorcerers.

The media does its best on a daily basis to showcase ridiculous stories in headlines until millions know the names of those involved. That's no different than turning a loud-mouthed, know-it-all, non-critical thinker such as Congresswoman AOC into a household name. The media shows her picture somewhere online every day. The latest stories revolve around her possible House ethics violations that are now the focus of a House Ethics Committee probe.

AOC's notoriety is not because of her legislative credentials. In fact, as of this writing and to the best of my knowledge, none of her bills have ever reached the floor of the House and thus have never been voted on. While she is a star on Twitter, she appears to be one of the least effective House members. I'm sure her family is proud.

Back to the Titans. Best they be shipped off to **Gitmo**, along with AOC, and locked away for life. Then the poor media execs will have a couple fewer celebs to write about.

An uncomfortable truth

Ready . . . aim . . . fire! Congratulations. You just shot yourself in the foot—not because you possess sharpshooter aim but more likely because the part of your brain tasked with critical thinking has this sign hung on its door: "GONE FISHING." It seems that critical thought, prudence, and discretion are permanent vacations.

Here are some things to ponder: students posting *how to cheat* videos on TikTok; students wondering why they were expelled from school; teenagers posting intimate videos for friends and those videos somehow making their way to family and clergy; politicians taking money from foreign agents and far-left organizations that want to remake our country into a Socialist paradise like Cuba or Venezuela. **HAS EVERYONE GONE BANANAS?**

As kids, we stood for the flag, recited the *Pledge of Allegiance*, and respected our elders, the military, and our institutions. No more. Nationwide riots break out. Crimes are committed by career criminals, who are processed and released back out into the community with no bail requirement. Police are vilified by the press and far left politicians. And we sit here and wonder why our country is sliding into anarchy. Daily, the media parade the worst humanity has to offer. Why do we need dozens of stories for every murder, robbery, and arson?

NOTABLE AND QUOTABLE

A big mouth don't make a big man.

—John Wayne, The Cowboys (1972)

I think the destructive, vicious, negative nature of much of the news media makes it harder to govern this country, harder to attract decent people to run for public office.

—Newt Gingrich, former Speaker of the House of Representatives

People I meet today, especially journalists who interview me, are astonished to hear that Lenin told me, in effect, that Communism was not working, and that the Revolution needed American capital and technical aid.

—Armand Hammer, former CEO Occidental Petroleum,
and philanthropist

Memo #41

The byproduct of unlimited on-line pages is the reporting of absolute garbage

It is bewildering to me

A casual scan of daily media shows no fewer than ten articles daily reporting on transgender issues; and they are not just reporting facts because there are woefully few of those. It's mostly one side blasting, shredding, taunting, and berating the other side. Now mind you, these articles are not buried on page fifty-two under the update on the Route 495 construction project. They are plastered on the front page—as if there was nothing more important to report on.

While the percentage of transgender folks in the country is reported to be somewhere in the neighborhood of 0.5 percent, the fact is that there are more articles on transgender issues than on North Korea, and those folks hate our guts and would like nothing more than to nuke us back to the Stone Age. So, the question that comes to my mind is this: Why? Why are so many mainstream media platforms placing this issue front and center? What is driving the probable 1,000 percent increase in the reporting and visibility of these stories? Answer: the media is playing the stories over and over again so as to desensitize the American public to the issue and that it is now considered "normal"—which it ain't.

The uptick in trans themed articles can partially be traced back to the ill-conceived and ill-considered Budweiser commercials that feature some young something—man woman, or in between is my guess. People lost their minds over this. Budweiser stock has plunged in value, and folks are forsaking Budweiser for the manlier can of Coors. I think the country has lost its collective mind.

Interestingly, I emailed the above paragraphs to a distant relative of mine and asked whether she felt these remarks were *worthy of inclusion* in this book. I anticipated a short yes or no response.

Below is her answer with a resounding agreement.

As you know, the media is backed by wealthy left-winged idiots. They just want to report on this crap to convince the people that there is such inequality, discrimination, and racism in this country when the leaders of our government are causing it to happen. They want to spew this narrative so the left can get votes to remain in power, and unfortunately, the people of this country are stupid enough to believe it. I think they are letting in all the migrants at the border for votes as well. They're willing to sacrifice people's lives and citizens of their own country from fentanyl coming in and killing our kids, and allowing murderers, terrorists, rapists, and human traffickers in. The risk is worth it to them! This is what happens when you give the government too much power! It hasn't gotten bad enough yet. When we have another 9-11 or a war breaks out, maybe people will finally wake up!

Mind you, I asked my relatively simple, binary question. The response I received, which I agree with 100 percent, is way more than I expected. And I am grateful that I am not the only one with this point of view. I suspect there are many of us, but most opt for a life of quiet desperation rather than letting their opinions be known. *If there is any hope of changing this narrative, we can no longer remain silent.*

That means engaging on the local level, becoming involved in community efforts to sweep those on the far left of our school boards, our city councils, and municipal offices. If you know people who voted these folks into office, engage them in conversations and enlighten them as to the consequences of their actions. Do so in a non-violent way. Just like your mother cautioned: use your words. Use persuasion and back up your augments with facts. Ask parents if they think it is OK for pornographic books to be available in their fifth grader's school library.

Byproduct of unlimited online news pages is reporting absolute garbage

Online websites have an advantage over paper-and-ink periodicals. For example, the *New York Times*, the *Washington Post*, and others have a finite amount of time to complete an issue and a finite number of pages on which to display all the articles, ads, opinion columns, and stories.

Not so for online media where the number of pages is virtually unlimited. Often these web pages are referred to as *real estate*—and the amount of real estate on Fox.com, or other leading online media platforms appears to be an unlimited number of pages that can magically be updated and expanded at will during a twenty-four-hour news cycle.

Some days I am forced to consider why I continue reading the day's online news at all. I'm convinced that news editors would spend some serious time figuring out the placement of news stories in a physical newspaper (e.g., the president on page one, the border issues on page two, Paris Hilton on page six, etc.).

A byproduct of the unlimited scrolling page counts available to *online* news sources is that stories that would never find their way into an actual newspaper end up being displayed after you have swiped down on your phone eighteen times. Such is the case with a "news" article from the *New York Post* dated April 29, 2023,[50] written by journalist Brooke Kato. In paragraphs too numerous to count, she tells the story of a Miami woman who shared a horrid experience as a three-part series on TikTok discussing how her roommate borrowed her vibrator and it was *so crazy* she had to move out.

Were I the owner of the *New York Post,* I would fire the editor who green-lighted the inclusion of the story and use it as an example to all other employees that they are in the business of reporting *news.* This story is a poor example of a human-interest feature, and the *New York Post* should be ashamed of itself for reporting it. It is absolute garbage, and that's where it belongs—in the garbage.

Expand the authority of the sergeant-at-arms

The sergeant-at-arms of the House and the Senate are to be the chief law enforcement officers of their respective legislative chambers. I would like to see their authority expanded and to be issued bars of soap, so that when a senator lies through their teeth, or a Congressperson deliberately lies about the opposition, the sergeant-at- arms would have full authority to have the offender pinned against the wall at the front of the chamber for all to witness, and have their mouth washed out with soap.

So that way, when a liberal Democrat lies in front of their colleagues and is then reported to the media about Republican efforts to strengthen border security and spins it so that the Republicans are actually gutting border security, they can look forward to a mouthful of soap and humiliation, televised for millions to see on the 6 p.m. news. I call that balanced reporting.

He thinks " YEA! Release them all, anywhere but Delaware."

Media reports on AOC–almost on a daily basis

Have you noticed how big corporate media goes out of its way to pump out almost daily stories about and big pictures of Congress-woman Cortez? Known mainly by her nickname, AOC, this media personality is often spoken of—and rightfully so—as one of the least-effective members of Congress. You may want to ask yourself why big media pumps out story after story highlighting a pretty, intellectually vapid, far-left, liberal Democratic member of Congress.

Remember the old saying, tell a lie often enough, and everyone starts to believe it? Well, folks who are reading today's media see Ms. Cortez in the news almost on a daily basis and thus think she is an important voice. My view is that this is exactly what America doesn't need, AOC pontificating on what she would do to right all the wrongs in the U.S. and show us how intelligent she is after attending Boston University and working as a bartender.

I thought secret messages went out with Watergate

It doesn't take a brain surgeon to understand that I am a conservative Republican. Yet I am not a fan of some of the communication tactics used by the Republican Senatorial Committee. For example, I received a text recently (I hate texts) that said, "The Republican Senatorial Committee has sent you a secret message. Please review within the next fifteen minutes." Secret message? Really? And yes, I promptly deleted it, in case you were wondering. The last time I received a secret message I was seven years old, and my friend John and I were hiding behind rose bushes on opposite sides of the street with our five-dollar walkie-talkies our parents bought for us at Woolworths!

NOTABLE AND QUOTABLE

Asking the current crop of Socialist liberal Democratic members of Congress to craft an intelligently designed legislative bill that protects our southern border and limits illegal immigration is like expecting a world-class BBQ chef to provide a five-star dining experience armed with nothing but gunpowder, a screwdriver and a cow.

—Unknown

A great many people think they are thinking when they are really rearranging their prejudices.

—Edward R. Murrow

Memo #42

The gray-haired Socialist standing on a soapbox (again)

The gray-haired Socialist standing on a soapbox (again)

Do you have a soft spot for weary old Socialists? I don't. You might have heard when Senator Bernie Sanders, surrounded by union officials *and no doubt standing on a soapbox*, demanded that the federal minimum wage be lifted, not to fifteen dollars per hour but to seventeen dollars per hour. And Sanders goes on to speak about the forty-hour workweek as if that number is sacrosanct and written in stone. For the record, I have never known anyone who is financially successful who worked forty hours per week. Success often comes with every hour worked over forty.

Sanders' Socialist economic policies, backed by big labor, fails to recognize that millions might lose their jobs as a result of the unintended consequences of such ideas becoming law. If I were an owner of a mid-level restaurant, I would much prefer to place a menu/iPad at every table to facilitate ordering and save on the cost of unneeded employees. I could save on benefits and not have to pay someone seventeen dollars per hour minimum wage. As an added bonus, the electronic order taker does not call in sick, steal time to watch TikTok videos of cats water skiing, or graze on free food all day long. And something else to contemplate–some jobs are NOT worth seventeen dollars per hour.

The continued argument conveniently omits the idea of value. Is sweeping the floor *worth* seventeen dollars per hour? Is a factory job placing part A into the hole on part B *worth* seventeen dollars per hour? Is standing at the front of a big box store as a greeter *worth* seventeen dollars per hour? Were I Walmart, I would place a robot clown with a happy face at the front door to greet everyone who walked by. For a few dollars extra, it could be programmed to tell you that acne cream for your teenager is in aisle seven.

If you think that would not be the case, let me remind you that when I grew up, we had gas station attendants to pump our gas at every station. Today, you will have to travel far and wide to find some-one to pump your gas. Everyone has been accustomed to pumping their own gas for years. If memory serves me right, New Jersey is the only state in the union that prohibits motorists from pumping their own gas, arguing that for safety reasons, a professional should be in charge of filling your tank! Oregon recently changed their seventy-two-year-old law that prohibited motorist from pumping their own gas. To think that ordinary folks could pump their own gas without blowing themselves up is beyond the grasp of New Jersey's intellec-tually challenged state lawmakers. Of course, New Jersey is among the bluest high taxed states in the Union. No surprise there.

I kid you not this is your Navy

I would like to sit down with the naval officer who green-lighted an active-duty second-class yeoman ***drag queen*** to be the new poster child for the U.S. Navy. Supposedly, he (?) is key to the Navy's recruitment drive to attract a talented and diverse workforce in the digital age. What a load of crack. And by the way, Vice Chief of Naval Operations Adm. Lisa Franchetti told the House Armed Services

Committee that the Navy is projected to fall 6,000 recruits, or 16 percent, short of its fiscal year 2023 goal for enlisted sailors.

Well now, I can see why the Navy is HOT to recruit non-binary, trans community recruits to fill its ranks. I do not agree with the decision, and my sense is that the officer who approved this should be thrown overboard from the deck of an aircraft carrier. A recruit in any branch of the military is expected to fight, and if necessary, die protecting their country, not to put on drag shows and show others how great they look in a stunning sequin evening gown and high heels.

My love-hate relationship with Fox News

Let me tell you why I am no longer a raving fan of media giant Fox News. It seems that every time I access Fox online, one of the very top headlines, often in huge letters, is about a trans person, a trans activist, or a trans something or other. Fox's lead story revolves around the one-half of 1 percent of the country who identifies as transsexual. Obviously, that doesn't count the almost 40 percent of college students who from time to time answer polls that they identify as bisexual, trans, or non-binary.

Growing up in Manhattan in the 1960s, I learned that 40 percent of something, 40 percent of damn near anything, is pretty damn close to 50 percent or HALF. If you can tell me with a straight face that nearly half of college kids identify as bisexual, trans, or non-binary, I'll gladly pay you for a bridge in Brooklyn.

Obviously, it's Trump's fault!

I seem to remember many of my friends and colleagues securing mortgages during President Trump's term of office. The rates on thirty-year fixed mortgages were in the range of 1.875 percent to 3.25 percent—under President Biden, the rates have escalated to as high as 8 percent as of this writing. Now to be fair, a lot has happened over that period of time, least of which is the magic of *Bidenomics* and the Fed raising short-term interest rates month after month.

I am certain that beyond a shadow of doubt, the *Teflon Biden Administration* will find a way to blame this on Donald Trump. The alternative is to admit to the American people that the policies of Biden's administration have had dire economic consequences for the majority of Americans.

How can you not be worried about America?

Democratic leadership policies at the highest level have assisted and enabled illegals to disappear into the interior of the country—calling it the *non-citizen movement initiative*—but there are actually midnight secret airplane trips arranged by federal authorities to go to regional airports without notification to local authorities. I have read numerous articles detailing these *ghost flights* arranged by government officials, published by the *Washington Times*, NBC, CNN, the *New York Times*, the *New York Post*, the *Washington Examiner*, the Daily Wire, and others.

What has transpired is tragic and, by many accounts, a gross violation of federal law. It's no surprise that border states are fighting the feds in court. Friends tell me they receive dozens of letters monthly from Conservative politicians asking for donations to help stop the mass illegal migration. Copies of personal letters from governors, senators, and members of Congress all have the same message: help us stop this massive scourge of illegals pouring into America.

I received one such letter, which riveted me in my seat as I read it. It was dated November 16, 2022,[51] and was addressed to the President of the United States, written by Texas Governor Greg Abbot. In big, bold, red letters across the page was the word COPY. I will share some of the letter with you here.

Dear President Biden:

The U.S. Constitution won ratification by promising States, in Article IV, § 4, that the federal government "shall protect each of them against Invasion." By refusing to enforce the immigration laws enacted by Congress, including 8 U.S.C. § 1325(a) (1)'s criminal prohibition against aliens entering the United States between authorized ports of entry, your Administration has made clear that it will not honor that guarantee. The federal government's failure has forced me to invoke Article I, § 10, Clause 3 of the U.S. Constitution, thereby enabling the State of Texas to protect its own territory against invasion by the Mexican drug cartels.

Your inaction has led to catastrophic consequences. Under your watch, America is suffering the highest volume of illegal immigration in the history of our country. This past year, more than 2 million immigrants tried to enter the country illegally, coming from more than one hundred countries across the globe. . . .

By opening our border to this record-breaking level of illegal immigration, you and your Administration are in violation of Article IV, § 4 of the U.S. Constitution. . . .

In more than 240 years of our great nation, no Administration has done more than yours to place the states in "imminent Danger."

I highly recommend that you read the letter in its entirety. You will find it with a simple internet search.

Personal pronouns and then some

Imagine my surprise when I read that the world of pronouns was much larger than I had imagined. Little did I suspect that in addition to he, him, they, her, etc., there lurked some of the following:

- Interrogative pronouns
- Emphatic pronouns
- Possessive pronouns
- Indefinite pronouns

And there are more that I won't list. Suffice it to say, I'm a pronoun boob, not realizing that my (mis)understanding barely scratched the surface of the term. Mind you, I couldn't define any of these if I stood on my head, balanced on an encyclopedia.

Kamala: The early days

Seems I never tire of writing about my least favorite, least effective vice president. Recent media reports have taken to reminding us of her early career, as the arm candy of the powerful San Francisco politician, Willie Brown. Mind you, the sixty-year-old Mr. Brown was still married, though separated, and enjoying his special relationship with Ms. Harris, going so far as to appoint her to a lucrative spot on the California Medical Assistance Commission. Interestingly enough, Kamala Harris possessed no medical experience that would have qualified her for the position.

At the time, Mr. Brown was the Democratic Speaker of the California State Assembly. Brown then reportedly appointed Ms. Harris to the California Unemployment Insurance Appeals Board. I would bet even money that Ms. Harris's career benefitted immensely from her boyfriend's patronage, just a hunch.

Another 4 million dollars of tax-payer funds wasted

Media reports indicate that the Biden Administration has provided roughly 4 million dollars to fight (alleged) ties between child labor in Nepal and climate change. Seems this falls under the heading of socially inclusive research—whatever that is. My guess is that gender equity gets mixed in as well. To say that the Biden Admiration's priorities are misplaced is a grand understatement—they are, in fact, absurd. Perhaps the $4 million could be better spent repairing roads and schools in America? Whatever became of prudent fiscal management and the responsible use of taxpayer funds?

In case you missed it

The National Archives—you know, the repository of our nation's history—has begun providing warning statements of potentially harmful content, citing that some records may be difficult to view as they may not express inclusive and diverse language. Documents such as the Declaration of Independence, the Constitution, and the Emancipation Proclamation might be too much for sensitive folks to deal with. I can say this has gotten way out of hand, but I sense you already know that. Might the gift shop slap stickers on reproductions of our most sacred documents with a warning that states: Content may be harmful to progressive liberals? My guess is that as you read the Constitution with your grandkids, you will not provide a warning label or disclaimer.

An unearned paycheck while striking

Yes, the media surprises me every now and then with a really crazy story. Leave it to a wise group of Democratic lawmakers in California to propose that unemployment benefits be extended to striking workers. The benefits would likely be provided by California's Unemployment Insurance Program. Mind you, the *fund* is reportedly 18 billion dollars in debt, but hey, it's California, what would you expect?

Don't auction off unfinished parts of the border wall

Yes, that is exactly what the Biden Administration is doing. Rather than finishing the southern border wall project and protecting our country, our brain-dead leadership has decided to auction off all the unused parts. When we finally elect leadership with brains, we—you know us taxpayers—will have to buy this stuff all over again.

Speaking of the southern border

The media reported in August 2023 that illegal border crossings at the U.S.–Mexico border rose 33 percent in July 2023, according to U.S. Government figures. I wonder what that number would be if we had, you know, say it with me, *a completed border wall?* At what point will the Biden Administration realize the immense damage they have inflicted on our nation?

But the President said…

In Sept of 2022, President Biden stated that the pandemic is over. Yet recent media reports indicate that some colleges are still mandating COVID-19 vaccines for students. Evidently, the folks running these schools did not watch the interview where the president stated, unequivocally, that the pandemic was over.

NOTABLE AND QUOTABLE

Citizenship is the right to have rights.

—Justice Earl Warren, fourteenth Chief Justice
of the Supreme Court of the United States

**In the first place, we should insist that if the immigrant
who comes here in good faith becomes an American
and assimilates himself to us, he shall be treated on an
exact equality with everyone else, for it is an outrage
to discriminate against any such man because of creed,
or birthplace, or origin. But this is predicated upon the
man's becoming in every facet an American,
and nothing but an American.**

—Theodore Roosevelt, twenty-sixth President of the United States

Memo #43

Thoughts on entitlement, equality, air, and opportunity

Oh my, college is too hard

Seems a large number of college students are of the opinion that college is harder than it should be. In fact, some call it a barrier to success and stressful. And, in this age of *work from home in your underwear*, many complain about old-fashioned professors insisting on classroom attendance. Really? I'm pretty certain that they would want to do away with deadlines as well because they are inconvenient.

Yes, I can write an entire book trashing the beliefs of these students, and I have news for them. Life—and a financially successful and rewarding life at that—is difficult. And life has deadlines. If you doubt that, tell your feelings to the IRS, your boss, the folks who send you jury duty notices, or when you are served with an arrest warrant, subpoena, or divorce papers. Let those folks know that you don't appreciate strict requirements or participation, or that it's overly difficult or inconvenient at this time, and you would appreciate it if they would be more flexible.

I suspect that courses in civil engineering, cybersecurity, aeronautics, and particle physics are more challenging than introductory psychology, sociology, political science, and ceramics. The coursework is hard because new concepts of science and math are unknown to most, and require intense study to grasp and understand them. A degree in civil engineering may prepare someone to build bridges or help erect a one-hundred-story office building. I would hope that the coursework is challenging and detailed enough to provide the needed knowledge to complete these types of projects safely. A cybersecurity expert has most likely had hundreds if not thousands of hours of study under their belt—a server at Olive Garden, probably not.

Stop whining, and start studying . . .

Oh, and as for overly difficult coursework, if particle physics were easy, everyone would be a physicist and show their straight A's to mom and dad. It is difficult to produce critical thinking, foster the ability to study long hours, and increase participation in the learning process—something these twits don't understand. Perhaps they should trash school altogether and instead take that Door Dash job where they could schedule their own hours. Of course, they may find that occasionally they have to work at an inconvenient time and ask for more flexibility because it is overly difficult.

For what it's worth

If I had the choice of sitting down with King Charles III of Great Britain or billionaire Bruce Wayne, aka Batman, I'd choose Batman.

> **Rich people make lots of money;**
> **wealthy people sign their checks.**
>
> —author unknown

A doctor once asked Ol' Blue Eyes (Frank Sinatra) how he felt in the morning after drinking so much Jack Daniels. His reply: "I don't know. I'm never up in the morning."

Thoughts on entitlement, equality, air, and opportunity

You are entitled to **air** and **opportunity**. Everything else comes at a price. I suppose if you find yourself in a forest, you may be *entitled* to berries and spring water as long as you stay ahead of bears. It might be blasphemy, but a college education comes at a cost. You are not *entitled* to a college education on the taxpayers' dime. Someone has to foot the bill to pay the professors, turn on the lights and heat, mow the lawns, maintain the buildings, and keep the student union cafeteria full of food. Ask the soybean farmer in Indiana how they feel about footing the bill so you can attend the university and earn a useless liberal arts degree that provides no useful skills. The farmer works eleven hours a day to feed their family and provide a better life for their children, not to underwrite your taking Intro to Sociology classes graded on a curve. But it doesn't stop there.

The media is chock full of stories about equality and entitlement. One of the more interesting stories I have been following is about the California State Legislature voting to provide billions in reparation money to African Americans even though California was never, to my knowledge, a slave state. I've read that African Americans are entitled to the money because of how they and their ancestors have been treated in America. While I don't pretend to understand every issue involved in this debate, if I were a reasonably successful tax-paying Californian, I would make haste to exit the state for a more fair-minded state where my hard-earned tax dollars are spent in a wiser fashion to benefit all citizens of the state, not any one group to the detriment of the others.

Should *you feel* that we should all be equal—as in a Socialist state where the government provides free housing and education for all, along with the guarantee of a job—then perhaps America should institute a 70 percent income tax rate applicable to all, rich and poor alike, with no write-offs, tax loopholes, or special considerations. Everyone would pay 70 percent of their income to the government, no matter their income level. And hey, there can be equality and poverty for all.

Opportunity provides a pathway to achievement, not a guarantee of attaining it. And to my knowledge, you can breathe as much **air** as you like. It's on the house.

Thank you for protecting our republic

I'm coming back to Judicial Watch as I believe their work exemplifies organizations we need more of, and that we owe them our support.

I quote from their mission statement directly:

Judicial Watch is a conservative, nonpartisan, American educational foundation that promotes transparency, accountability, and integrity in government, politics, and the law. Judicial Watch advocates high standards of ethics and morality in America's public life and seeks to ensure that public officials do not abuse the powers entrusted to them by the American people.

I smiled as I reviewed their May 2023 bulletin in which they reported yet another important milestone in their efforts to remove ineligible voters from election rolls in state after state. Cleaning up the rolls of states' eligible voters is an important step in deterring election fraud, and the numbers reported are eye-opening, compelling, and meaningful.

We all read of charges of massive election fraud in the presidential election between Trump and Biden. How much actual fraud occurred, if any, is anybody's guess. After reading dozens of articles on the subject, I came away with more questions than answers. Was there subterfuge, manipulation, dirty tactics, or possible illegal activity? I don't discount the possibility, but for every charge leveled, there was a court that dismissed the charge. So, what are we, the American people, left to believe? I'm not sure, but I have become distrustful of the election process, which is why I am grateful to organizations such as Judicial Watch that appear to have my back and yours.

Los Angeles County was directed to remove 1,207,613 ineligible voters in a lawsuit settlement with Judicial Watch. Folks, that's more than 1.2 million voters who were removed from the lists that LA County had previously refused to remove. Among those on the list were people who had moved out of the state, non-citizens, and those who had died.

That comes on the heels of another Judicial Watch victory where New York City was directed to remove 441,083 ineligible names from their voter rolls. Ditto for North Carolina that had to remove 430,000 ineligible names.

Three states and over **2 million** ineligible names removed from official voter rolls—that's a tremendous number, and yet it represents only three states. Imagine how many more millions of people are on the rolls of the other forty-seven states. So, here's the $64,000 question: Why must states be sued in federal courts to compel them to do what they should lawfully do?

I applaud and support Judicial Watch in its work to reduce the very real risk of election fraud. Thank you!

Which article of the Constitution says that?

Here's something from an article on the *American Thinker* website, published on July 8, 2023.

Karine Jean-Pierre: Racial Preferences Are an 'Important Constitutional Right'
By Thomas Lifson

Employing the euphemism "affirmative action," President Biden's press secretary claimed that there is a constitutional right to receive preferential treatment based on one's race. She was discussing recent Supreme Court decisions on MSNBC with host Ari Melber and made the extraordinary claim without citing any language in the Constitution—because of course there isn't any to support her and, contrarily, language in the 14th Amendment that prohibits it. . . Of course, the media will never ask where in the Constitution is there a right to racial preferences or "affirmative action." I suppose that is part of the preferences that she enjoys in her job. (Emphasis added.)[52]

Wow! This makes me wonder if the White House press secretary ever actually read the United States Constitution. And if she has, would she please point my way to the paragraph that enumerates the right she speaks of? I have a copy of the pocket Constitution, and I'll get her one to carry in her purse or pocket so she can check the facts before opening her mouth.

Early on in her job, she told everyone who would listen that she is the first immigrant Black woman and the first openly LGBTQ person to serve as White House press secretary. Personally, I don't care what color she is, who her father was, what side of the tracks she grew up on, or who or what she likes to have sex with. That's her business, and it should not be the business of the White House press room podium. There is a time and a place for everything, and her standing on her soapbox to announce her firsts to the world—well, it was neither the time nor the place.

Don't tell anyone about the Soros money until after I'm elected president

Seems Vivek Ramaswamy, one of the many presidential contenders for the 2024 Republican nomination, has gone out of his way to deep-six his connection to the Soros family. Evidently, this fellow felt a need to take an almost six-figure grant from a Soros family foundation to attend law school. You might remember that billionaire George Soros funds left-wing causes and funds many liberal district attorneys in the country who elect not to prosecute crimes. In addition, he throws millions of dollars to every liberal cause from Oregon to California, to Illinois to Vermont. Any candidate who takes Soros family money is on my eternal shit list and will NEVER receive my vote.

NOTABLE AND QUOTABLE

**The function of economic forecasting
is to make astrology look respectable.**

—John Kenneth Galbraith, noted economist and author

**I have left orders to be awakened at any time in case of
national emergency, even if I'm in a cabinet meeting.**

—Ronald Regan fortieth President of The United States

Memo #44

There must be a better way to spend American taxpayers' money

Biden's picks

Should the American people be crackbrained enough to elect Mr. Biden as president for a second term, they will surely get what they deserve. Here is my somewhat skewed view of how important positions within the administration and cabinet will be filled—by whom "*his people*" believe are qualified candidates. Keep in mind that extra consideration is given to extreme left-leaning Democrats; oppressed minorities such as transgender-non-binary humans, extraterrestrials, dangling participles, and others.

Choice for Secretary of Defense—Former Chicago Mayor Lori Lightfoot

Choice for Secretary of State—DHS Secretary Mayorkas

Choice for Secretary of the Treasury—Senator Bernie Sanders

Choice for Secretary of Homeland Security—White House Press Secretary Karine Jean-Pierre

Choice for Director of the FBI—Whoopi Goldberg

Choice for Chairman of the Federal Reserve Board—Congresswoman AOC

Who knew?

I took a gander at the May 5, 2023, edition of *The Jerusalem Post* and ran across something I had never ever heard of. The headline in the Business & Innovation section read, "Haredi Towns to Receive 'Kosher Electricity' in New Energy Ministry Plan."[53]

Now I'm familiar with kosher wine, kosher meats, and the like. But kosher electricity? That's a new one for me. And it begs the question, is there kosher coal, gasoline, or nuclear power? If so, what does a rabbi have to do to ensure it is kosher? No disrespect, just saying . . . .

Climate hysteria = mental anxiety

Vice President Kamala talking about climate anxiety, and how young people are thinking they don't want to bring children into such a world is beyond ludicrous, yet she takes to the stage slinging preposterous sludge against the wall to see what sticks. What will the climate be like if I buy a home? Really, does she come up with this crap on her own or does she have a staffer invent this BS while sitting in the comfort of their air-conditioned office? Stay tuned as Team Biden, in their last desperate act before being kicked to the curb of history attempts to ban air conditioners because we are addicted to cool air and comfort. Facts and evidence be damned. Air conditioning is NOT an addiction. They are practicing fear on steroids, trying to convince Americans that we must drastically alter our way of life or the planet will die by two Septembers from now.

Meanwhile, Bill Gates, the noted climatologist (ha ha) is reported to have said that the planet is fine and there's a lot of climate exaggeration going on. Seems that might be a nice way of saying that liberal Democrats are actually lying to the American public as they seek to ban more and more of our household appliances. Where does it end? Do we sit in sweltering homes in August, reading by candlelight and walking everywhere?

Well, it ain't the police academy anymore

As a student at PS 40 and Junior High School 104 in lower Manhattan, I often spent time with my buddy John. For years we hung out at each other's homes, sharing meals as our moms set an extra place at the dinner table. He lived two blocks west of the schools, and I lived two blocks to the east. When I "graduated" from sixth grade, I got to walk twenty-five feet across the street to start seventh grade at JHS 104.

Between school and John's apartment was the New York City Police Academy. True to its name, that was where the NYC Police Department trained all its new officers. The street was always clogged with squad cars and crowds of rookie cops grabbing coffee, going to classes, the pistol range, or lunching at the hot dog carts that lined the street. For an 11-year-old kid, there was no safer place in the city than 20th Street between 2nd and 3rd Avenues. The street was literally blue from end to end with a sea of smartly starched uniformed patrolmen.

So, imagine my surprise when I read that "hundreds of migrants are to be housed in NYPD's former Police Academy building."[54] Leave it to the *New York Post* in the May 5, 2023, edition to bring back my memories of the police academy. I'm pretty certain that the city outgrew its old training facility and built a new one somewhere else, but the thought of housing hundreds of illegals so close to two big NYC public schools for first grade through ninth grade seems outrageous to me. *Why place so many people who knowingly and deliberately broke our laws so close to our children?*

I said it before, and I'll say it again—the folks who run New York City are imbeciles and should be tossed out on their collective asses and replaced with intelligent, reasonable, conservative-minded, thoughtful, law-abiding public servants.

Who talked Biden into this trans gift?

The May 2, 2023, edition of the *Washington Examiner* got under my skin, and this is not the first time. After reading a story by Luke Gentile,[55] their Social Media Producer (whatever that is), about President Biden offering a half-million-dollar grant to help teach English to **Trans Pakistani Youth**, I sped to the trusty internet to find out some facts about Pakistan. For example, I knew they were always at odds with their neighbor India, and that both of them are armed to the teeth. What I did not know was Pakistan has the third largest English-speaking population on the planet with over 100 million speaking English. Why on earth our esteemed leader felt that *trans youth* needed a basket of federal dollars to improve their English is beyond me.

It seems there are better ways to spend American taxpayers' money. Perhaps Biden will be willing to make a personal charitable donation to this cause and claw back the taxpayers' money to the U.S. Treasury. I don't think so, but I thought I would send the idea out into the universe and see if anything comes back. One last observation. I wonder who talked Biden into this trans gift. I highly doubt that he came up with it on his own.

Paterson Public Schools should be ashamed

When someone is passed over for more than forty promotions, there has to be a reason, and it's usually not a good one. In the case of Thomas Franco, a New Jersey educator, he insists in a lawsuit that he was passed over for promotions repeatedly because he is white. Here is the headline: "N.J. Educator Applied for 45 Promotions and Got None Because He Is White, Lawsuit Says."[56] The story, written by Anthony G. Attrino, appeared in nj.com on April 28, 2023.

According to the lawsuit filed on April 21, 2023, "Nearly all administrative level positions within the Paterson Public Schools, greater than 95 percent are held by Black and Hispanic individuals." The lawsuit alleges that many of those hired had less experience and lacked the academic credentials Franco possessed.

It is wrong to discriminate based on race and skin color, no matter what the skin color. This educator persisted in trying to advance his career despite ingrained discrimination, and finally he had to reach out to the judicial system to provide the freedom for advancement that should be available to everyone based on merit. My hope is that the courts will dispense justice and not judicial discrimination.

Why am I not surprised?

It's probably common knowledge that a former aid of Congresswoman Cortez (AOC) has been elected leader of the New York Communist party. Bet her parents are delighted and proud of her tweets. Ms. Justine Medina identifies as a Marxist (no surprise there).

My hope is that New Yorkers will wake up to the *New York Daily News* or the *New York Post* with a headline that has two things in the same sentence—AOC and Communist. Perhaps that will put an end to the city's love affair with the bartender/Congresswoman.

New tax deduction for the well-connected? There are media reports that according to a whistleblower, there are alleged deductions of thousands of dollars made to sex clubs and prostitutes on Hunter Biden's federal income tax returns.

Mind you, the **whistleblower** in question is an anonymous IRS criminal investigator. Stop for a moment and understand that this is a very specialized unit of the IRS. Here is the intriguing job description of an IRS criminal investigation special agent, taken directly from the IRS website:

Who are we?

Criminal Investigation (CI) is the law enforcement branch of the IRS. Our mission is to serve the American public by investigating potential criminal violations of the Internal Revenue Code, and related financial crimes, in a manner that fosters confidence in the tax system and compliance with the law.

As a Special Agent, you will combine your accounting skills with law enforcement skills to investigate financial crimes. *Special Agents are duly sworn law enforcement officers* who are trained to "follow the money." No matter what the source, all income earned, both legal and illegal, has the potential of becoming involved in crimes which fall within the investigative jurisdiction of the IRS Criminal Investigation. Because of the expertise required to conduct these complex financial investigations, IRS Special Agents are considered the premier financial investigators for the Federal government.[57]

I understand this to mean that the individuals who are stepping up to tell the truth, under oath, are not some garden variety finance majors from State U. These are highly trained professionals associated with an elite unit of the Internal Revenue Service.

Now, back to Hunter. We all can't be as well-connected as President Biden's son, Hunter, who appears to have the inside track on some really interesting tax deductions. It would have been fascinating to have been a fly on the wall as Hunter met with his tax professional and recounted deduction after salacious deduction. Who knew that sex clubs and prostitutes were tax deductible? Perhaps he listed them under professional services or miscellaneous deductions.

Of course, as of this writing, the sexy deductions are alleged. Might there be some actual proof in a sock drawer somewhere?

Madness the new normal?

Back in October 2023, protesters marched on the home of Seattle Mayor Bruce Harrell, angry that the liberal city mayor had proposed adding $17 million to the police budget for the crime-ridden city. Worse yet, the protest occurred on the mayor's birthday.

Seattle Police Department reports that violent crime is at a fifteen-year high, yet protesters want to see the police budget cut. When did rational thought become the exception? Should a protester's home be vandalized, or worse yet, their parents mugged, my guess is that they would desperately be calling 9-1-1 and angry that they are put on hold, due to understaffing in the police department and its budget shortfalls.

NOTABLE AND QUOTABLE

It will be of little avail to the people that the laws are made by men of their own choice if the laws be so voluminous that they cannot be read, or so incoherent that they cannot be understood.

—James Madison, fourth President of the United States, Father of the Constitution

Memo # 45

Media polarizing the country? You don't say...

I love it when billionaires feud!

Elon Musk badmouths George Soros (with GOOD reason).
Mark Cuban criticizes Elon Musk.
Elon Musk condemns Jeff Bezos.
Mark Zuckerberg taunts Elon Musk.

Why do we so thoroughly enjoy seeing folks with billions and billions of dollars squaring off against each other? One reason is that they possess power few folks have—to use their money and influence to effect BIG change. For the rest of us, it may provide exciting entertainment. It reminds me of *Lifestyles of the Rich and Famous*, the old TV show where Robin Leach took us into the mansions, yachts, private planes, and lives of the super-rich.

We love to stick our noses into billionaires' lives—like a car accident you just can't stop looking at! The reason we have rubbernecking on the highways is because people cannot tear themselves away from seeing the carnage. I find it fascinating, kind of like King Kong taking a swing at Godzilla. Hey! Pass the popcorn and get ready for a wild ride.

By the way, you need to look no further than *Forbes, Fortune,* or the *Wall Street Journal* to get an upfront and enthralling view of billionaire families' internal warfare. It really is a sight to behold, complete with the threat of being written out of grandfather's will.

Exactly what skills are taught in college?

Robert Kiyosaki's book *Why the Rich are Getting Richer* made mention of an interesting cover headline appearing in the August 2016 edition of *Consumer Reports* magazine. The headline shouted, "I Kind of Ruined my Life Going to College." The article's focus was how student debt was ruining the lives of millions. Students graduated with a degree and still did not know how to do anything worthwhile. Life skills were largely absent, as were basic financial skills. Colleges turned out kids with diplomas that were useless to a wide swath of employers. No wonder so many graduates became disillusioned over how they would ever pay off their student loans when they were qualified to do very little.

Having attended a four-year state college and majoring in the *social sciences*, I can attest to the fact that I left college *skill-less*. While I would love to blame the state, the college, the state regents, and others, the fault lay squarely with me since I did not select classes that would teach and strengthen hard skills that would be useful once I entered the real world of career and employment.

I graduated knowing little, if anything, about career advancement, dressing for success, personal finances, taxes, saving for retirement, basic banking, goal-setting, wealth creation, and understanding leases and rental agreements. While many around me graduated with student loans, college credits in the "Stone Age" (the 1970s) were affordable, and my only debt was revolving credit. Still, I saw friends who told of crushing debt loads for their master's programs and other advanced degrees.

Were I in charge of college curricula, the first three semesters would be 100 percent life skills taught by accomplished and successful professionals, not by assistant professors spouting academic theory from a textbook written by a colleague. By the time graduation came along, writing resumes and charting a career path would be as natural as putting on shoes and brushing teeth—a far cry from today's useless bachelor's degrees.

Social media kills brain cells

There has been a never-ending parade of stories and articles that social media for youngsters should be regulated and that it causes actual harm to kids' brains. In fact, some media outlets have come out and said what any reasonable person would suspect; namely, that constant and never-ending use of social media is harmful to people's health.

This reminds me of the lies and justifications by the tobacco industry when they insisted there was no link between lung cancer and smoking. I'm pretty certain that we will soon see a headline that contains the words, *what did they know, and when did they know it?*

You don't have to be an astronaut to notice all the millennials with their eyes glued to their phones, catching up on every post from every person they hardly know. I'm told that it is not uncommon for them to spend upward of five hours a day or more on social media.

Remembering back when I was a tween (a preteen) and my mom said to go out and play—well, **we all went out and played**. We played stickball, basketball, and baseball. We rode our bikes and skateboards, and threw a football around. Today, kids sit on a bench—sedentary, eyes glued to their phones, barely speaking to each other. What's worse is that kids seem overly concerned about what others are saying or not saying about them. And don't get me started on the worst of the worst—cyberbullying and sexting. What is most concerning to me is the long-term effects this will have and the problems that will present themselves over time.

Tired old Democrat wanted for store greeter position

I think Congressman Jerry Nadler should apply for a store greeter position. He is imminently qualified. Despite his claims of collusion between President Trump and Russia being disproved by the Durham report, the tired old Democrat clings to his untrue narrative like a cocaine addict clinging to an empty spoon. He is everything anti-Trump. Whether the facts support him or not is completely irrelevant. It's time he hung up his Congressional cape and took a spot on the wooden stool at the entrance to Walmart, greeting customers all day long with that tired old grin.

It's news to me

I didn't get the memo. There is a Taylor Swift economy, and no one told me. It creates hundreds of millions in revenue. Hey, I'm old. I've heard of the underground economy, I've heard of the welfare economy, and I've heard of the Republican and Democratic economies. But I have never heard of the Taylor Swift economy. Even the Beatles, The Who, and the Rolling Stones did not have their own economies. One can only hope that a band of smartly armed IRS agents are following Ms. Swift around the country from venue to venue, ensuring that, as Elizabeth Warren is fond of saying, she pays her fair share in taxes.

We don't care what parents want

I don't know, maybe I'm old fashioned, but I believe that local school boards should embrace and reflect the will of the parents who send their kids to the local schools. So, pardon me if I was astounded to learn that 84 percent of parents are opposing the teaching of gender identity in sex-education classes. I fully agree with the article by Mike Miller posted on the *Red State News* website on July 5, 2023.[58]

Seems the school board is fine with allowing boys and girls to take the classes together. The leftists on the school board are hell-bent on relabeling boys and girls as an unlimited number of genders, and shoving equity, inclusion, and diversity down everyone's throats. This is the liberal radicalism on steroids.

It seems that Fairfax County, Virginia, and its neighbor Loudoun County are hell-bent on prioritizing Diversity and Equity Inclusion (DEI) in the classroom, as well as teaching critical race theory. I may be wrong, but I believe more than one hundred articles have been written about the school boards in these two Virginia counties. The best outcome: parents will throw these DEI imbeciles out on their asses and elect representatives who are in line with parental attitudes. Of course, parents can always pull their children out of the offending schools and leave empty classrooms for school boards to fight over.

By the way, I think 84 percent is an overwhelming majority.

Of pizza ovens and grenade launchers

A headline on the *American Thinker* website caught my eye and chilled me to the bone.July 11, 2023

China readying for total war, America laser-focused on pronouns and wood-fired pizza ovens

By Eric Utter[59]

Mr. Utter writes that while we in the West are concerned with bathrooms, pizza ovens, pronouns and mis-gendering people, China is teaching young school children to play with fake knives, grenade launchers, guns, and rifles. Mind you, Chinese citizens are prohibited from owning the real version of these weapons to protect themselves and their families, but the government wants to indoctrinate the next generation to know the weapons of war they will use to fight the West. In other words, *get 'em while they're young.*

Caption: My father told me "Don't take this job" I should have listened!

The Secretary Should Have Stayed Home

The Secretary of Energy should have stayed home. Jennifer Granholm, the boss of Team Biden's Energy Department, went on a goodwill tour, complete with staffers and reporters, to spread the cheer about electric vehicles and toe the party line. If you missed the NPR story headlined "Electric Cars Have a Road Trip Problem, Even for the Secretary of Energy," you missed a good story. Apparently, the wagon train (excuse me, the EV train) had problems locating charging stations along their route. Mind you, this was a four-day trip from North Carolina to Tennessee. The idea was to draw attention to the Green New Deal and the billions of dollars the administration is spending to electrify automobile transportation.

The Secretary and her staff had a brutal blast of reality when they found there were not enough charging spots on their route through Georgia. To make matters worse, her staffers blocked a charging spot with their gasoline-powered vehicles—a BIG no-no. A family who was denied the charging space on this sweltering hot day—a family with an infant in the car—ended up calling the police to get these government bureaucrats to move their cars. That's what happens when you hire a horse's ass to do the job of a thoughtful and intelligent person.

NOTABLE AND QUOTABLE

I've heard that progressives hate old people, one reason why they are always trying to shove aside and discredit older colleagues with more wisdom than they have.

—Rodger Friedman

Once a government is committed to the principle of silencing the voice of opposition, it has only one way to go, and that is down the path of increasingly repressive measures, until it becomes a source of terror to all its citizens and creates a country where everyone lives in fear.

—Harry S. Truman

Memo # 46

Teachers engaging in poisonous anti-American activities?

A practical alternative to woke media

I'm old enough to remember many trips to the dentist's office as a kid with yet another cavity in need of *drillin' and fillin'*. While sitting in the waiting room, I always looked forward to reading the ol' dog-eared copies of *Popular Mechanics* magazine. As a teenager, not much interested me besides girls, science stuff, some sports, and, oh yeah, girls. The magazine was chock-full of cool stuff such as futuristic robot battle tanks, Mars landers, and lasers. I viewed it as the bridge between *Star Trek* and what was possible. It was both cool and interesting. And I admit that on more than one occasion, I swiped the magazine and shoved it under my coat to continue reading it on the subway ride back home. Dr. Stern would never miss it.

So, imagine my surprise some 50 years later while sitting in the dentist's waiting room that I happened upon—you guessed it—a copy of *Popular Mechanics*. I was so intrigued with the articles that I sent in the subscription card and, with a nostalgic smile on my face, waited for my first issue to arrive.

I was not disappointed. In the first ten minutes of reading, I discovered the following:

- Why ancient Roman concrete is so strong (who knew, right?)
- If we'll ever reach *warp speed* (hey, I'm all in on this one)
- A research publication titled *Classical and Quantum Gravity*
- 389 ways train derailments can occur (okay, who did the counting here?)
- How we'll die on Mars

Anyway, you can see why I'm hooked for life and look forward to countless hours of discovering stuff I don't know. It sure beats the constant drivel the media cooks up every day! Not a spot of politics, woke happenings, or inane banter from the Secretary of the Treasury, Senate majority leader, or Vice President of miscellaneous.

My take on the student loan debacle

To all the student loan borrowers out there: Hi, I'm an American taxpayer. I work for a living. And if you've been waiting for the government to pay off your student loan, you can stop waiting. The Supreme Court invalidated President Biden's scheme to buy your votes with cash. I'm not paying. So, do whatever you have to do. Cancel your Netflix subscription, shop at The Dollar Store, buy store brand cola or get a second job. But YOU WILL pay off the debt that you agreed to. It is not my responsibility!

Wash your mouth out with soap Fairfax, VA.

I received a letter from *The James Madison Institute* requesting a donation. There was a cover letter from my Florida Senator, Marco Rubio. I was stunned to read the following:

English classes in Fairfax, VA indoctrinate students by playing *Woke Bingo,* which forces students to see if they are *privileged.*

Here are some of their markers of privilege:

- Having your own bedroom
- Having married parents
- Having a parent in the military
- Being a native English speaker

Why would teachers engage in such poisonous anti-American activities? To quote Florida Governor Ron DeSantis, *"We won't allow Florida tax dollars to be spent teaching kids to hate our country or to hate each other."*

I couldn't agree more.

After a bit more reading, I found the following in the Institute's website:

MISSION: Our mission is to tether the Sunshine State to the wisdom of free-market capitalism, limited government, the rule of law, economic liberty, and the principles that have made our nation great.[59]

Now that's something I could get behind.

Why do you place your trust in the media?

I long ago turned away from the *New York Times.* It seems that its tagline—"All the News That's Fit to Print"—has, in my opinion, morphed into "All Our Liberal Opinions in Print." I learned long ago that the job of the journalist is to inform the public, not attempt to sway public opinion with bias and innuendo.

I agree with Jacob Sullum article published in *Reason* on April 27, 2020.

Here is the headline:

When It Comes to Covering Trump, *The New York Times* Has Abandoned Any Distinction between Reporting and Opinion[61]

And, I salute and agree with the *Washington Times* for their accurate reporting of journalistic bias that seems to know no bounds. How editors in positions of authority place their stamp of approval on trash posing as news I'll never understand. Look at this headline by Jennifer Harper, the *Washington Times*, October 27, 2020:

Broadcast Networks Deliver 92 percent Negative Coverage for Trump, 66 percent Positive for Biden: Study[62]

Seven-four million disagree with you, Mr. President

Mr. Biden makes no secret of the fact that he is out to "protect democracy." Were he to read *The Federalist Papers*, written long ago by Alexander Hamilton, James Madison and John Jay, he might have a better understanding of just what a democracy is. But our esteemed president seems to not have the time for rational thought.

He spends his days signing dozens of executive orders that countermand the will of Congress.

You see, in round numbers, there were about 74 million people who voted for Mr. Trump in the 2020 Presidential election. Those 74 million disagreed with the ideas, policies, and opinions of Joe Biden. On a daily basis, we have seen how Mr. Biden ignores the will of those who don't agree with his viewpoint. His politics and policies are like a cancer that has spread across America.

No matter which side of the aisle you sit on, you can't help but see the poisonous character of this American president.

A little bit about the seeds of crazy

For a country to exist and thrive, many ingredients must come together in just the right way to ensure that the citizens of that country, their children, and their children's children have a shot at a bright and secure future. There are those serving in Congress, among them members who have labeled themselves the Squad, who seek to crash our country into a brick wall. With ideas such as open borders, the dismantling of the Customs and Border Patrol, free education, free medical care, subsidized public housing, and guaranteed income for those who unlawfully enter our country, these legislators would gleefully steer America to financial ruin.

Imagine if we were to provide free money, benefits and entitlements to the millions of people sneaking across our borders. The seeds of our eventual ruin are contained in these ideas. A country on the brink of financial ruin serves no one. The Squad's solution? Dismantle capitalism and raise taxes to unheard of levels. Confiscate assets of those who have been successful and, redistribute all wealth.

And, one more ingredient. Teach poisonous theories in our schools. Create a curriculum that teaches critical race theory, the 1619 Project, that you are racist because you are white or that there are dozens of genders and that taxpayers should foot the bill for gender-reassignment surgery, that boys can play on girls' sports teams, and they should use one dressing room for team sports and that they share bathrooms. Within a short span of years, these ideas will become normal and mainstream. Talk about the seeds of crazy.

This is not my America. These are the seeds of Crazy. These are the seeds of self-destruction. This has to stop now.

In their eyes, divided we stand, united we fall

Liberal politicians are fond of seeking to provide special entitlements to groups of people who they view as disadvantaged. That's why African American farmers and ranchers were targeted for gifts of taxpayer funds that other races did not qualify for.

Waiting for the hysteria to begin

A sensible and long overdue bill introduced by House Republicans has the potential to stop election fraud in its tracks. *The American Confidence in Elections (ACE) Act,*[63] is designed to restore voter confidence in the elections process. The bill includes the following:

- A photo ID requirement to cast a federal election ballot

- Bars non-citizens from voting

- Requires annual maintenance of voter rolls

- Prevents mailing of unsolicited ballots to rolls that have not been maintained.

Now all we have to do is wait for the liberal Democratic chorus that will accuse the Republicans of having the audacity to write a bill that is racist, unfair, demeaning to minorities and the LGBTQ+ community. I'm not sure how they will justify their words, other than shouting, protesting, and arguing that the bill is yet another example of a fascist government. Personally speaking, I would like it explained to me just how election integrity is racist, and why non-citizens should not be excluded from having a vote in Federal elections. So, I wait for the hysteria to begin.

NOTABLE AND QUOTABLE

Give me your four-year-old's, and in a generation,
I will build a Socialist state.

—Vladimir Lenin, Founding Head of the Soviet Union

People always have been, and they always will be stupid victims of deceit and self-deception in politics.

—Vladimir Lenin, Founding Head of the Soviet Union

They don't subscribe to our sense of morality; they don't believe in an afterlife; they don't believe in a God or religion. And the only morality they recognize, therefore, is what will advance the cause or Socialism.

—Ronald Regan, fortieth President of the United States

Memo #47

Spiteful and petty is not the proper role of government officials

How can I not comment on this?

Ron White once said, "I had the right to remain silent . . . but I didn't have the ability."

I know how he felt. As I read the daily headlines, I see absurd, hateful, and biased headlines most everywhere I look. Here is my take on recent court decisions.

I disagree with CNN often. I recall feeling that AOC must be deranged if she believes that Supreme Court justices are destroying the legitimacy of the court because they decide cases without consulting her first. Such was the case with Biden's Student Loan plan being deemed against the law.

AOC chimed in that the Biden Administration went back to the drawing board after the Supreme Court denied them the ability to forgive student loans. She told the media that *she was unsatisfied* with the terms of the new Biden plan. Well excuse me, Miss Congresswoman, sorry to hear you are unsatisfied. She went on to say, **"I would like to see** interest payments suspended during this time, especially during that 12-month ramp-up period." This is from the

Thinking " WOW! This $174,000 Congressional salary sure beats bartending!

clown who tells us it's rough getting by on a $174,000 Congressional salary while she drives an electric Tesla around town.

Well, Sandy, I would like to see you go back to being a bartender. I would also like to see you agree to debate either Senator Cruz or Ben Shapiro. You have spurned their invitations. As you consider yourself a learned legislator, perhaps it would be helpful for the entire country to see how truly ignorant you are. And by the way, Sandy, there are not three chambers of Congress. Every school kid knows there are two—hence the term *bicameral legislature*.

Since when is spiteful and petty the proper role of government officials?

I get it. I wasn't born yesterday. Politicians feud with each other all the time. Some manage to make it an art form. Witness the spite and pettiness of former New York City Mayor Bill de Blasio. The media was all over it when the City of New York decided to paint "Black

Lives Matter" on the street right in front of Trump Tower. Newspapers portrayed it as a battle between a powerful and loved mayor and a corrupt president.

In fact, the mayor joined activists in painting the huge yellow letters on 5th Avenue between 56th and 57th Streets. The mayor reportedly said, *Let's show Donald Trump what he does not understand. Let's paint it right in front of his building for him.* The only reason the mayor of New York City did that was to piss off the president of the United States, Donald Trump. There was NO OTHER REASON.

We need to move some crude oil—got a pickle jar?

As reported by Oil Price.com on September 28, 2023, in a story written by Charles Kennedy, seems Exxon has some offshore oil platforms in California that are designed to feed crude oil to refineries. Some years back, in 2015, a pipeline near Santa Barbara split and caused a substantial oil spill. Due to strong local opposition, the pipeline was never fixed and is no longer in operation.

What's interesting, to me at least, is that during September of 2023, Judge Dolly Gee, a Los Angeles judge, refused to overturn a county decision that prohibits the company from using tanker trucks to transport the crude oil. As the Santa Barbara Board of Supervisors denied a transport permit to Exxon, the company has no choice but to shove the oil in the back of station wagons, backpacks, pickle jars, coffee cans, and other assorted means to move the oil from where it is produced to where it is refined. Alternatively, Exxon can tell California to pound sand, sell all their assets in the state, and let these folks start using campfires to keep warm at night.

NOTABLE AND QUOTABLE

Yes, all the quotes below are attributed to Joe Biden,
the life-long politician who Americans
voted into the White House.

During a campaign rally in 2008, in Missouri, Joe Biden
asked the audience to stand up and clap for State Senator
Chuck Graham. "Stand up, Chuck, let 'em see you,"
Biden said, gesturing for Graham to stand. State
Senator Chuck Graham is a paraplegic, confined
to a wheelchair following a car accident.

Or how about this?

"No ordinary American cares
about their constitutional rights."

Or

"I never had an interest in being a mayor 'cause
that's a real job. You have to produce. That's why
I was able to be a senator for 36 years."

Or

"The next person that tells me I'm not religious, I'm going
to shove my rosary beads up their ass."

Or

"Banning guns is an idea whose time has come."

The fact that these comments came from the leader
of our country, the commander of our Armed Forces,
is shameful, sad, and pitiful.

Is there a fingerprint kit in the house?

You have to be living under a rock not to have heard that a bag of cocaine was found in the Biden White House. What I find ABSURD is the media kidding around about it. Even I didn't expect the media to joke about this. Naturally, the thought crossed my mind that perhaps the troubled son of a sitting president with a known history of drug abuse might come forward and admit he lost it while horsing around in the West Wing. No such luck. But it occurs to me that someone from the Secret Service, the FBI, Denny's, or Victoria's Secret might have a fingerprint kit that can be used to lift prints off the baggie. Wouldn't it be grand if there was a 99.9 percent match to Hunter B?

I would love to see how the Democrat-loving media would spin that story!

Making blood donation more inclusive?

Why didn't I know this? Evidently there are those within the LGBTQ+ movement that are seeking to make blood donations more inclusive. How the LGBTQ+ agenda inserts itself into the blood donation process is beyond me. Ultimately, I expect the Red Cross to be called a racist organization that promotes white supremacy.

Influencer? I think not

I don't get it. I read that an **influencer**—whatever that is—is a self-proclaimed title. Or does a certifying authority grant that title after 10,000 hours of study in the subject of influence? I digress. I read that an influencer—*with a beard and broad shoulders*, you know the type—he can bench press 185 pounds and terms himself gender fluid. What the hell does that even mean? Does he sport testicles during weekdays and ovaries on the weekend? Does he dress up in a chiffon dress for Sunday afternoon tea? How about jock strap and short shorts for rugby practice on Tuesday nights, and then beers with the guys at the local pub? In my America—the one where we remember to stand for the Pledge of Allegiance, respect and support the military, recite the National Anthem at ballgames, and you are what you are the day you were born—you don't get to choose.

It seems that America has become distracted with this nonsense. The louder some idiot shouts, the more attention they get, even if they have nothing useful to say.

The dimwitted politicians of New York now condone and support multiple genders on birth certificates, over and above male or female. Beware if you don't have your pocket guidebook of acceptable pronouns. I guess *inoffensive speech* is when a police officer under fire screams into their radio that they are taking fire by an unknown, genderless, non-binary person wearing a hoodie, and they need assistance. Then again, New York hasn't made a logical decision in years, one of the reasons I left decades ago.

Be grateful you are NOT in New York City but be mindful that you are an American in an America that has seemingly lost its collective mind. Tread carefully.

What does this Congressman know that we don't?

Congressional testimony from Rep. Tim Burchett (R-Tenn.) opened a Pandora's box of UFO secrets and his quote that aliens have technology that could "turn us into charcoal briquette." I ask you, does this sound like a guy making stuff up or someone who's privy to ultra-classified intelligence? And yes, the charcoal briquette line was a really nice touch—scary but a nice touch.

Tell us how you REALLY feel

I have not set foot in Denver, Colorado in many years. I think the last time was when I was suffering a temporary mental setback and cast my vote for Jimmy Carter for president. Turns out that was one of my darkest days, but psychotherapy was not needed. But during 2023, the *Denver Post* ran an opinion piece by Jo Ann Allen on the front page of its online edition on July 7, 2023.[64] The subject of her rant was Donald Trump. Now I'm open to other folks' opinions, but hey, when a major newspaper prints trashy opinions with words such as Sociopathic, Narcissistic, and Racist in the headline, I tend to get hot under the collar.

Yes, it's fascinating how ultra-leftist liberals conveniently ignore facts, twist facts, and mold the world to their vision of who is right (them, all the time) and who is wrong. Ms. Allen lets it all hang out—throw him in prison for a really long time because I disagree with everything he stands for.

Well, Ms. Allen, it appears **you do not stand for**:

- Strong and secure borders
- Intelligent immigration policies
- A strong military free of diversity, equity, and inclusion (DEI) indoctrination
- Low inflation
- Modest budget deficits
- Strong standing in the international community
- Low interest rates
- Unifying the country rather than tearing it apart

My biggest fear is that these folks will somehow manage to place Mr. Biden or, worse, Mr. Newsom or Ms. Harris in the White House for four more years of ABSURD governing.

NOTABLE AND QUOTABLE

To those critics who are so pessimistic about our
economy, I say: "Don't be economic girlie men!"
The U.S. economy remains the envy of the world.
We have the highest economic growth of any of the
world's major industrialized nations. Don't you
remember the pessimism of twenty years ago
when the critics said that Japan and Germany are
overtaking the U.S.? Ridiculous! Now they say
that India and China are overtaking us. Now
don't you believe it! We may hit a few bumps—
but America always moves ahead.
That's what Americans do.

—Arnold Schwarzenegger, Republican National Convention Speech,
August 31, 2004

Afterword

A friend of mine had suggested that I name this book **America**: *Eyes Wide Shut.*

He insinuated that our country was sleep-walking through a nightmare, and many were intent on seeing how bad, bad can get. He is not wrong. *What is remarkable is the speed of the downward trajectory of the U.S. under President Biden.* What's worse, is media bias and favoritism has been right there fanning the flames of discord and discontent, and worse yet, they are not above printing mistruths.

Media bias is evident in many of the stories I have written about in this book. You have only to read through a portion of them to spot the bias. You will notice scarcely a quote from the *Washington Post* or *New York Times*; the reason is that I become highly skeptical of the accuracy of the news reported those publications. Mind you, I grew up with the *New York Times,* and during my decades in the Washington, D.C. area, read the *Post* regularly.

Yet the media is not the only one to blame for the sad state of America. The current cast of characters occupying seats of power makes me wonder if the electorate is high on crack cocaine and if they will ever come to their senses. I know folks who stumped for Biden, stuffed envelopes, and *manned the phones.* I wonder if they are happy with how things turned out. Reminds me of the old quote, *Be careful what you wish for.*

My mission as an author is to help inspire Americans to steer our country back on to a sensible path envisioned by our founders and enshrined in our Constitution. I wrote this book to raise awareness of what is sorely wrong with America today. While many would seek to cast blame, **the fault lies squarely with us**, the Americans who voted the current slate of politicians into office. Whether a school board, a city council, a state legislature, a governor, a mayor, the House of Representatives, the Senate, or the presidency. The buck stops here. The buck stops with us. **The fault, America, is our own.**

We have allowed haters to run our country—haters of Democracy, haters of Capitalism, haters of fairness, haters of personal responsibility. Our weak-willed populace cast their votes for politicians offering ever-increasing handouts, subsidies and entitlements.

People on both sides of the political aisle are passionate when speaking of entitlements. My view of entitlements is rather simple. We are all entitled to air and water. If you find yourself in a forest, you can add nuts and berries to my short list. Everything else must be earned, purchased, or paid for by someone. Entitlements have become the cocaine of politics and have swayed the minds and opinions of people who should know better.

This country was not founded on ever-increasing entitlements. It was founded on the rights of the individual, states' rights, and limited federal government. The colonists were fearful of a powerful king, and took great pains to devise a form of government that would guard against the tyranny so evident in their former homeland. Today, the federal government has reached into every facet of our lives, regulating everything in sight. They want to dictate the kind of stove you use to cook your eggs, the lawnmower you use to mow your yard, how you heat your home, and the car you drive.

The progressive leftist policies of the Democratic Party want to use your tax dollars to enrich the lives of illegal aliens. Need I remind you that the first action these illegal aliens took upon entering America was to commit a felony. They want to provide cradle-to-grave entitlements that will lure greater and greater numbers of illegals to our shores while bankrupting our nation. Their hope is that those individuals, given citizenship, will permanently vote for Democratic candidates over at least the next one hundred years. *The lives of your children and grandchildren are at risk, as well as yours.*

America, it's time to wake the hell up and repair our broken country and get off the pathway to hell. The gut-wrenching decline of our country is real and chronicled daily in our media. Please, for your children's sake, and the sake of your children's children—become involved, vote and say a prayer for America.

Divided, we all fall, the question is, can we recover?

I think that the former Speaker of the House of Representatives put it succinctly:

We're at the crossroads. Down one road is a European centralized bureaucratic socialist welfare system in which politicians and bureaucrats define the future. Down the other road is a proud, solid, reaffirmation of American exceptionalism.

—Newt Gingrich, former Speaker of the U.S. House of Representatives

God Bless The USA

The end or not. It's up to you...

Citations

1. "Meet the Economists."The Fed—Meet the Economists.Accessed October 29, 2023. https://www.federalreserve.gov/econres/theeconomists.htm.

2. Big Oil incurred record loss in 2020 | *Oil & Gas Journal.* Accessed October 29, 2023. https://www.ogj.com/general-interest/economics-markets/ar- ticle/14197855/big-oil-incurred-record-loss-in-2020.

3. June/July 2022 *Forbes Magazine.* "The Future of Work. How the pandemic reshaped the way we work, learn and live. Plus, the world's most powerful women, the best places to travel and the secrets of successful entrepreneurs." https://www.forbesmagazine.com/product-page/june-july-2022

4. Tucker, Jeffrey A."The Economic Disaster of the Pandemic Response.*"Imprimis*, December 5, 2022. https://imprimis.hillsdale.edu/the-economic-disaster-of-the-pandemic-response/.

5. "Watch: Elon Musk Interview with Ron Baron in NYC [Full Video]." Tesla- North.com, November 4, 2022. https://teslanorth.com/2022/11/04/watch-elon-musk-interview-with-ron-baron-in-nyc-full-video/.

6. Smith, Kyle. "Millennials Need to Put Away the Juice Boxes and Grow Up." *New York Post*, March 22, 2016. https://nypost.com/2016/03/21/millennials-need-to-put-away-the-juice-boxes-and-grow-up/.

7. Ap. "Republicans Reject Jordan for House Speaker on First Ballot, but More Voting Likely." *Japan Today.* Accessed October 29, 2023. https://japanto- day. com/category/world/Republicans-reject-Jordan-for-House-speak-er-on-first-ballot-but-more-voting-likely.

8. Schilke, Rachel."Buttigieg Warns Looming Rail Strike 'would Not Be Good' for Economy."*Washington Examiner*, November 22, 2022. https://www.washingtonexaminer.com/news/buttigieg-warns-looming-rail-strike-not-good-for-economy.

9. "Part 4: Entire CNN Coronavirus Town Hall (April 16)." CNN, April 17,2020. https://www.cnn.com/videos/health/2020/04/17/entire-april-16-coronavirus-town-hall-part-4-sot-vpx.cnn.

10. "Io—Home." FSI.Accessed October 29, 2023. https://cyber.fsi.stanford.edu/io.

11. Vasquez, Whitney. "50 Cent Scores Small Victory in Penile Enhancement Fight after Judge Rules Lawsuit against Medspa Can Move Forward." *RadarOnline*, December 12, 2022. https://radaronline.com/p/50-cent- penile-enhancement-lawsuit-surgery-moving-forward/.

12. Moore, Tina, and Jorge Fitz-Gibbon. "Man Busted with 20,000 Fentanyl Pills Set Free: Police Sources." *New York Post*, November 14, 2022. https://nypost.com/2022/11/13/man-arrested-with-20000-fentanyl-pills-set- free/.

13. Goldsberry, Jenny. "Detransitioner Who Had Breasts Removed Says She Is Suing Doctors Who Approved Surgery." *Restoring America*, December 5, 2022. https://www.washingtonexaminer.com/restoring-america/fairness-justice/former-nonbinary-patient-sues-social-worker-therapist.

14. "A Just Society: The Embrace Act (2019—H.R. 5071)." GovTrack.us. Accessed October 29, 2023. https://www.govtrack.us/congress/bills/116/ hr5071.

15. Utter, Eric, "40 Percent of Students at Liberal Arts Colleges Now Identify as LGBTQ, Study Finds." *American Thinker*. Accessed October 29, 2023. https://www.americanthinker.com/blog/2022/12/40_of_students_at_ liberal_arts_colleges_now_identify_as_lgbtq_study_finds.html.

16. "Consolidated Appropriations Act, 2023 (2022—H.R. 2617)." GovTrack. us. Accessed October 29, 2023. https://www.govtrack.us/congress/ bills/117/hr2617.

17. Dear american job seeker—rickscott.senate.gov. Accessed October 29, 2023. https://www.rickscott.senate.gov/services/files/FE938C2F-152C- 47FA-A200-16BFE5573837.

18. Keene, Houston, FOX News. "A California City to Give Universal Income to Transgender, Nonbinary Residents Regardless of Earnings." FOX13 News | Seattle & Western Washington | Formerly Q13 News, April 5, 2022. https://www.fox13seattle.com/news/california-city-universal-income-transgender-residents?taid=624c8ab13225ef000128cf73&utm_campaign=trueAnthem%3A+Trending+Content&utm_medium=trueAnthem&utm_source=twitter.

19. Grabow, Colin and Lincicome, Scott, Cato.org. Accessed October 29, 2023. https://www.cato.org/blog/charge-all-past-present-members-cato-mer- catus-institutes-treason.

20. Hellner, Jack, "New Rules in the House Worry Democrat Leader Hakeem Jeffries." *American Thinker*. Accessed October 29, 2023. https://www. americanthinker.com/blog/2023/01/new_rules_in_the_house_worry_ democrat_ leader_hakeem_jeffries.html.

21. Taylor, Jessica, and Scott Detrow. "Bernie Sanders Launches 2020 President- tial Campaign, No Longer an Underdog." *Vermont Public*, June 1, 2021. https://www.vermontpublic.org/vpr-news/2019-02-19/bernie-sanders-launches-2020-presidential-campaign-no-longer-an-underdog.

22.   Masterson, Matt. "Chicago Tops 630 Homicides, 2,600 Shootings in 2022: Po- lice." WTTW News. Accessed October 29, 2023. https://news.wttw. com/2022/12/01/chicago-tops-630-homicides-2600-shootings-2022-police.

23.   Utter, Eric. "Democrat Rep. Sheila Jackson Lee Proposes Bill Criminalizing Po- litical Criticism of Minorities." *American Thinker*. Accessed October 29, 2023. https://www.americanthinker.com/blog/2023/01/demo- crat_rep_sheila_jack-son_lee_proposes_bill_criminalizing_political_criti- cism_of_minorities.html.

24.   Mondeaux, Cami. "Virginia Bill Would Consider Fetuses as Car Passengers in HOV Lanes." *Washington Examiner*, January 14, 2023. https://www. washingtonexaminer.com/policy/healthcare/virginia-bill-would-con-sider-fetuses-as-car-passengers.

25.   Stack, Megan K."Greece Turns Eye to Tax Evaders." *Los Angeles Times*, May 24, 2010. https://www.latimes.com/archives/la-xpm-2010-may-24-la- fg-greek-rich-20100524-story.html.

26.   "Sen. Joe Manchin on Debt Ceiling Debacle: 'We Have Not Been Fiscal- ly Responsible': Fox Business Video." Fox Business, January 18, 2023. https:// www.foxbusiness.com/video/6318855817112.

27.   "Sen. Cruz Introduces Constitutional Amendment to Impose Term Limits for Congress: U.S. Senator Ted Cruz of Texas." Senator Ted Cruz, Jan- uary 23, 2023. https://www.cruz.senate.gov/newsroom/press-releases/ sen-cruz-introduces-constitutional-amendment-to-impose-term-lim-its-for-congress.

28.   Utter, Eric. "University Offers 'Unconditional Love Fund'. . .as Long as You're Not Heterosexual." *American Thinker*. Accessed October 29, 2023. https://www.americanthinker.com/blog/2023/02/university_offers_uncon-ditional_love_fund_as_long_as_youre_not_heterosexual.html.

29.   Stauffer, Elizabeth. "Could Michelle Obama Become the Democrats' 2024 Presidential Nominee?"*Washington Examiner*, February 5, 2023. https:// www.washingtonexaminer.com/opinion/could-michelle-obama-be-come-democrats-2024-presidential-nominee.

30.   Janoski, Steve. "NYC Dominatrix Viktoria Nasyrova Convicted in Cheese-cake Poisoning Case." *New York Post*, February 10, 2023. https://nypost. com/2023/02/09/nyc-dominatrix-viktoria-nasyrova-convicted-of-at- tempt-ed-murder-for-poisoning-eyelash-stylist/.

31.   Utter, Eric. "23 Baltimore Schools, 2,000 Students: Not One Tested Pro-fi- cient in Math." *American Thinker*. Accessed October 29, 2023. https:// www.americanthinker.com/blog/2023/02/23_baltimore_schools_2000_students_not_one_tested_proficient_in_math.html.

32.   Grossman, Hannah, and Fox News. "District Abolishes Urinals for Mid-dle Schoolers to Appease Outrage on Transgender Bathroom Policies." Fox

News, February 12, 2023. https://www.foxnews.com/media/dis- trict-abolishes-urinals-appease-outrage-transgender-bathroom-policies.

33. King, Ryan. "Schumer Knocks GOP on Debt Ceiling: 'Where Is Your Plan, Mr. McCarthy?'" *Washington Examiner*, February 12, 2023. https://www.washingtonexaminer.com/news/senate/schumer-knocks-gop-debt-ceil- ing.

34. "Doe Awards FY23 Congressionally Mandated Sale of Crude Oil from the Strategic Petroleum Reserve." Energy.gov. Accessed October 29, 2023. https://www.energy.gov/ceser/articles/doe-awards-fy23-congressionally-mandated-sale-crude-oil-strategic-petroleum-reserve.

35. Fung, Katherine. "Majority of Biden's Cabinet Appointments so Far Are Obama Officials." *Newsweek*, December 22, 2020. https://www.newsweek.com/nearly-60-percent-bidens-cabinet-appointments-so-far-are-obama-officials-1556641?utm_term=Autofeed&utm_medium=Social&utm_source=Facebook&fbclid=IwAR0By9HpuS-E8r8VLqbCEkwWrMYZT_mbEsV76jUNabVzu6VUtzxj1kXx-JofI#Echobox=1608669883.

36. "Home—the Giving Pledge." Giving Pledge. Accessed October 29, 2023. https://givingpledge.org/.

37. Carnahan, Ashley, and FOX News. "San Francisco Considers Repealing Law That Boycotted Conservative States over Anti-LGBTQ, Abortion Legislation." FOX News, February 20, 2023. https://www.foxnews.com/media/ san-francisco-considers-repealing-law-boycotted-conservative-states-anti-lgbtq-abortion-legislation.

38. "The Florida Senate." Senate Bill 932 (2023)—The Florida Senate. Accessed October 29, 2023. https://www.flsenate.gov/Session/Bill/2023/932.

39. Martin, Ken. "Bank of America Totaled $1.2 Billion in Penalties, Settlements in 2022." FOX Business, February 24, 2023. https://www.foxbusiness.com/markets/bank-america-totaled-1-2-billion-penalties-settlements-2022.

40. Grossman, Hannah, and Fox News. "Arizona School Board Member Says District Should Reject Hiring Teachers with Christian Values: 'Not. . Safe.'" FOX News, March 3, 2023. https://www.foxnews.com/media/arizona-school-board-member-district-should-reject-hiring-teachers-with-christian-values-not-safe.

41. David Lawder, "Yellen says ending abortion access would be 'damaging' to U.S. economy, women," Reuters.com, May 10, 2022. https://www.reuters.com/legal/litigation/yellen-says-eliminating-abortion-rights-would-have-damaging-effects-us-economy-2022-05-10/

42. Utter, Eric. "Swarthmore College Catalogs LGBTQ+ Terminology." *American Thinker*. Accessed October 29, 2023. https://www.americanthinker.

com/blog/2023/03/swarthmore_college_catalogs_lgbtq_terminology. html.

43. Mondeaux, Cami. "Biden Asks Wealthy to Pay 'little Bit More' in Taxes to Avoid Medicare Insolvency." *Washington Examiner*, March 8, 2023. https://www.washingtonexaminer.com/news/white-house/biden-pro-poses-increase-tax-rates-to-extend-medicare.

44. Biden, Joseph R. "Joe Biden: My Plan to Extend Medicare for Another Generation." *New York Times*, March 7, 2023. https://www.nytimes.com/2023/03/07/opinion/joe-biden-medicare.html.

45. "Study Shows New York City Rats Carry SARS-COV-2." ASM.org. Accessed October 29, 2023. https://asm.org/Press-Releases/2023/March/Study-Shows-New-York-City-Rats-Carry-SARS-CoV-2.

46. May, Nina. "If We're Doing Reparations, Here's Who Should Pay Them." *American Thinker*. Accessed October 29, 2023. https://www.american-thinker.com/articles/2023/03/if_were_doing_reparations_heres_who_should_pay_them.html.

47. Equity language guide al al—sierra club. Accessed October 29, 2023. https://www.sierraclub.org/sites/default/files/sce-authors/u12332/Equity%20Language%20Guide%20Sierra%20Club%202021.pdf.

48. Laad, Rajan. "Another Self-Appointed Language Policeman Reports for Duty." *American Thinker*. Accessed October 29, 2023. https://www. americanthinker.com/blog/2023/03/another_selfappointed_language_policeman_reports_for_duty.html.

49. Brodow, Ed. "Diversity Executives—the U.S. Version of Soviet Political Commissars." *American Thinker*. Accessed October 29, 2023. https://www.americanthinker.com/articles/2023/03/diversity_executives____the_us_version_of_soviet_political_commissars.html.

50. Kato, Brooke. "My Roommate Borrowed My Vibrator—It Was so 'crazy' I Had to Move Out." *New York Post*, April 29, 2023. https://nypost.com/2023/04/29/my-roommate-borrowed-my-vibrator-i-had-to-move-out/.

51. Governor Greg Abbott—Office of the Texas governor. Accessed October 29, 2023. https://gov.texas.gov/uploads/files/press/BidenJo- seph_11.16.22.pdf.

52. Lifson, Thomas. "Karine Jean-Pierre: Racial Preferences Are an 'Important Constitutional Right.'" *American Thinker*. Accessed October 29, 2023. https://www.americanthinker.com/blog/2023/07/karine_jeanpierre_ racial_preferences_are_an_important_constitutional_right_.html.

53. Shalom, Yanon, Walla, Yitach. "Haredi Towns to Receive 'kosher Electricity' in New Energy Ministry Plan." *Jerusalem Post* | JPost.com, May 5, 2023. https://www.jpost.com/business-and-innovation/energy-and-in-frastructure/article-742202.

54. Celona, Larry, Joe Marino, Tina Moore, and Allie Griffin. "Hundreds of Migrants to Be Housed in NYPD's Former Police Academy Building." *New York Post*, May 5, 2023. https://nypost.com/2023/05/05/hundreds-of-

migrants-to-be-housed-in-nypds-former-police-academy-building/.

55.   Gentile, Luke. "Biden Offering $500k Grant Focusing on Teaching English to Trans Pakistani Youth." *Washington Examiner*, May 2, 2023. https://www.washingtonexaminer.com/news/biden-500k-grant-pakistan-transgender-youth.

56.   Attrino, Anthony G. "N.J. Educator Applied for 45 Promotions and Got None Because He Is White, Lawsuit Says." NJ, April 28, 2023. https://www.nj.com/passaic-county/2023/04/nj-educator-applied-for-45-pro- motions-and-got-none-because-he-is-white-lawsuit-says.html.

57.   "IRS Criminal Investigation Special Agent." IRS Careers, May 12, 2023. https://www.jobs.irs.gov/resources/job-descriptions/irs-criminal-inves-tigation-special-agent.

58.   Miller, Mike. "Virginia School Board Ignores 84 Percent of Parents Opposed to Teaching 'gender Identity' in Sex-Ed Classes." redstate.com, July 5, 2023. https://redstate.com/mike_miller/2023/07/05/virginia-school-board-ignores-84-percent-of-parents-opposed-to-teaching-gender-identity-in-sex-ed-classes-n771481.

59.   Utter, Eric. "China Readying for Total War, America Laser-Focused on Pronouns and Wood-Fired Pizza Ovens." *American Thinker*. Accessed October 29, 2023. https://www.americanthinker.com/blog/2023/07/ china_ready-ing_for_total_war_america_laserfocused_on_pronouns_and_ woodfired_pizza_ovens.html.

60.   "About Us." James Madison Institute, October 17, 2023. https://jamesma-di- son.org/about-us/.

61.   Sullum, Jacob. "When It Comes to Covering Trump, the New York Times Has Abandoned Any Distinction between Reporting and Opinion." Reason.com, April 27, 2020. https://reason.com/2020/04/27/when-it-comes-to-covering-trump-the-new-york-times-has-abandoned-any-dis-tinction-between-reporting-and-opinion/.

62.   Harper, Jennifer. "Broadcast Networks Deliver 92% Negative Coverage for Trump, 66% Positive for Biden: Study." *Washington Times*, Octo- ber 27, 2020. https://www.washingtontimes.com/news/2020/oct/27/ study-bi-ased-broadcast-networks-92-negative-trump/.

63.   Actions—H.R.4563—118th Congress (2023-2024): American confidence in. . . Accessed October 29, 2023. https://www.congress.gov/bill/118th-con-gress/house-bill/4563/actions?s=1&r=1&q=%7B%22search%22%3A%5B%2218%22%5D%7D.

64.   Allen, Jo Ann. "Opinion: Just a Brief Reminder of Trump's Nonsensical Ramblings." *Denver Post*, September 6, 2023. https://www.denver- post.com/2023/09/06/donald-trump-rambling-nonsense-arrest-georgia-quotes/.

Acknowledgements

While it doesn't take a village to birth a book and get it into the world, it does require many hands to help it along. I could not have accomplished this by myself. So, I want to thank all the friends, colleagues, and hired guns that made this book possible.

To my first line of defense, Sue Vander Hook, who scrubbed and polished each sentence of my Sunday Memo early on. She was great to collaborate with. Sue took a scalpel where needed and made certain I was not embarrassed by my lack of grammatical skills. Sue, I am eternally grateful.

To the talented team at Bradley Communications who supported my project with skill, patience, and the utmost professionalism. Thank you to Steve and Laura Harrison, Geoffrey Berwind, Cristina Smith, Christy Day, Debbie Englander, Val Costa, and Beth Volz. You have my gratitude and sincere appreciation.

My *first readers* provided valuable insights on the manuscript that I was blind to. Thank you, Michael Marks, Roger Due, John Butler, and Alla Kaluzhny. Your contributions improved this book in ways I cannot describe. Thank you again.

To Eric Utter, a superbly talented writer and contributor to *American Thinker* and Thomas Lifson, editor of *American Thinker* and all the terrific writers at American Thinker website, who so graciously allowed me to quote them in the book. Thank you so much for your generosity.

To my *hired guns* at Upwork, Valeryi, Tabakanov, my wonderful illustrator in the Ukraine, who took my ideas and magically turned them into forceful illustrations, Chelsey Mears, my tireless letter writer, and Kurt Beyers, who pieced together the many citations into a logical framework. Thank you all.

To my family, my wife Reena, and my kids Avery and Jason for putting up with me while I was glued to the keyboard. What started out as a one-page weekly memo to friends and family was transformed into this book.

To my mom and dad, who both passed many years ago, thank you for instilling in me the wisdom to speak out and not blindly follow when I see injustice.

To Dan Kennedy, who provided much wisdom and insight to me over the last decade. While I never sat on Dan's knee, learning life lessons, his guidance has been invaluable in my success. Thank you, Dan.

To the cast of characters in the Congress of the United States, The White House and various state capitols, who provided a never-ending supply of horrendous policies to comment on.

About the Author

Born and raised in New York City, Rodger is a former Senior Vice President of Morgan Stanley Wealth Management and a practicing Chartered Retirement Planning Counselor (SM). Rodger is a fiscal conservative who long ago was in debt up to his eyeballs. Frequent trips to the library, as well as reading over a hundred books a year, helped put him on the right path toward financial autonomy.

A graduate of State University of New York, he admits the worst use of his time, ever, was getting an undergrad degree in political science. A proud member of *Sons of The American Legion*, Rodger actively supports charities to assist first responders and military families. He and his wife Reena have two wonderful kids and live in Florida.

Rodger Friedman is available for speaking engagements and media interviews.